Thank You for purchasing this book!

Welcome to
Dr.

The Magic
How to Let Go of Other

Author, Lyn K
Certified Professional Coach

"My mission is to provide understanding, comfort, knowledge, wisdom and personal power in relationships."

www.GrowTrainingInstitute.com

Cover Design by Cal Sharp
www.Caligraphics.com

Published by www.GrowPublications.com
©2020

What others are saying about *The Magic of Detachment*

"Bright, smart, and interesting."
--Gilat, Amazon review

"Hi, Thank you for giving me the gift of your words in the book magic of detachment. I COULDN'T PUT it down all week and have gained so many empowering tools that have stayed in my thoughts daily. I RECOMMENDED IT TO A FRIEND. Having read so many books over the years I found this one very relevant and down to earth. You were obviously writing from experience and kept it real and workable. THANKS again. Look forward to reading more."
--Regards, Tracey Carter

Freeing!!! Enlightening!!! New hope!!
"I gave this wonderful book this rating because it has helped me see what I have been doing all these years. This booked has brought the spot light on many behaviors of mine and helped me understand how to be free of them. Must read, I think, for all people."
--Sandra, Amazon.com Review

I'm finally free!
"What an eye opener. I've finally have approval to be a B#tch! I'm cutting off feeling guilty. This books really helps appreciate self love. It's worth the investment."
--BDelicious, Amazon.com Review

"This is clear, concise information and advice for dealing with people, who drain our energy in all kinds of ways, that you can start applying today. I liked it so much, I bought 2 more copies for each of my daughters."
--Amanda, Amazon.com Review

"Dr. Kelley tells it like it is. I've read all of her books on relationships and feel I have grown by leaps and bounds due to her honest, straight, real information. She writes like she is talking to her best friend. All the strategies I've used so far that she suggests have worked for me! I feel so much more confident in dating now,

and I'm not wasting time with men who are wrong for me. This was worth more than 100 times the cost of the books to me. I highly recommend her books."
   --Tanya Murray, San Diego, CA

   "I am at the point of having a better understanding of what the author speaks because I have been journeying for a while in the field of psychology and self improvement as well as quite a bit of experience interacting with people.
   This is very good writing.
   Nothing is black and white. Yet this book is filled with formulas that I do intend to use to ease my journey called life. I thank the author because I was using a lot of those methods unconsciously now I can be more conscious in their use. One thing is clear though we cannot do it for others since our life is our primary focus. Each must take responsibility for him or herself."
   --By Life Is Good, Amazon.com Review

Dear Jane Series:
Book 1: *The 12 Biggest Mistakes Women Make in Dating & Love Relationships*
Book 2: *How to Cure a Commitment-Phobic*
Book 3: *How to Turn a Player into a Stayer*
Book 4: *Controlling and Manipulative Men: How to Spot Them and Handle Them*
Book 5: *Self-Centered and Narcissistic Men: How to Spot Them and Handle Them*
Book 6: *Addicted Men – Drugs, Alcohol, Porn and More: How to Spot Them and Handle Them*
Book 7: *Low Achieving Men - Passives, Wimps, Dreamers: How to Spot Them and Handle Them*
Book 8: *Cheap Men: How to Spot Them and Handle Them*
Book 9: *Men who Lie and Cheat: How to Spot Them and Handle Them*
Book 10: *Emotionally Unavailable Men: How to Spot Them and Handle Them*
Book 11: *The Romantic Terrorist: Protect Yourself from Stalking, Harassment, Bullying and Threats*
Book 12: *How to Get Any Man You Want to Want YOU*
Book 13: *The 10 Biggest Mistakes Men Make in Dating & Love Relationships*
Book 14: *How to Break Up, Survive and Thrive*
Book 15: *Bad Dick, Good Jane: How Good Girls Get Bad Boys to Behave, Fall in Love and Commit*

Other Self-Help Books by Lyn Kelley:
How to Stick With Your Diet & Exercise Program
How to Motivate People! The 3 Magic Keys to Unlock Anyone's Hidden Motivation
The 7 Self-Sabotages: Why People Sabotage Themselves and How to Stop It
How to Become Your Own Life Coach in 12 Easy Steps
Stalking 101: Everything You Need to Know to Keep Yourself Safe
How to Motivate Yourself: Secrets of the Motivational Superstars
Thousands of Angels: Your Path to Peace, Healing and Abundance
One Day She Woke Up and Decided to be Brave: A Woman's Journey from Fear to Courage

I offer telephone and email coaching.
Contact me to set up an appointment!

lyn@janesgoodadvice.com

Learn more about Dr. Lyn and Relationship Coaching
www.janesgoodadvice.com

Follow Dr. Lyn:
Facebook: http://facebook.com/ lyn.kelley1
Twitter: http://wefollow.com/JanesGoodAdvice
LinkedIn: http://www.linkedin.com/in/drlynisin

See Dr. Lyn's YouTube videos:
The Biggest Mistake Women Make in Dating and Love Relationships:
http://youtu.be/--aGjh3WgPc

Is He a Commitment Phobic?:
http://www.youtube.com/watch?v=cLCqQHzmNOA

How to Stick With Your Diet and Exercise Program:
http://youtu.be/SEJvHJkKtSM

Bad Dick, Good Jane
http://www.youtube.com/watch?v=QYQenwJdfW4

Magic of Detachment
https://www.youtube.com/watch?v=bUSsaTq6Clo

Controlling and Manipulative Men
https://www.youtube.com/watch?v=gc6LGkonSr8

Emotionally Unavailable Men
https://www.youtube.com/watch?v=yXUBBE7MgLo

Self Centered & Narcissistic Men
https://www.youtube.com/watch?v=5lMDvDF2r1o

The Magic of Detachment
How to Let Go of Other People and Their Problems

By Lyn Kelley, Ph.D., CPC
Certified Professional Coach

Table of Contents

Introduction: What Does It Mean to Detach?
How I Stopped Being a Whipping Post
Recovering People-Pleasers
I Just Want to Feel Good
What Is Detachment?
Highly Sensitive People
Detached Concern
It's Not Easy – But Worth the Work

Chapter One: It's not Them, It's YOU
How to Protect Yourself from Other People's Problems (OPP's)
What's Really Wiping out All Your Energy
If One More Person Tells Me They Need Me I Will Scream!

Chapter Two: The Seven Toxic People in Your Life
Baiters
Haters
Emotional Vampires
Controllers
Manipulators
Moochers
Drama Addicts
The 11 Best Ways to Manage Toxic People
How to Treat a Snakebite

Chapter Three: Me, Then You
Your Unalienable Right to Pursuit of Happiness
Are You Putting Yourself Last?
Validators vs. Invalidators
Why Others Sabotage Us and How to Handle Them
How to Handle Criticism without Anguish
Choose Your People Well

Chapter Four: Your 4 Guiding Forces
Lead With Your Head
Trust Your Gut
How to Use Your Chi
Your Invisible Suit of Armor
Follow With Your Heart
Why You Worry and How to Stop It
10 Tips for Handling Anxiety
Navy Seals Stress Relief Tactics

Chapter Five: Embracing Detachment
Why Detach?
How to Detach
The 3 Main Obstacles to Detachment and How to Overcome Them
Letting Go of People from our Past
Debbie Downers

Chapter Six: How to Confront Your Tightest Bonds
You Are Not Them
Co-Dependency
Co-Dependent Meets Narcissist – The Bad Match
Co-Dependency vs. Empathy
The Cure: Respect, Reality and Reciprocity
Enabling
Actual Helping Behaviors
Boundaries That Promote Intimacy
Stop the Insanity!
Get Fed Up!

Chapter Seven: When to Do When You've Reached Your Breaking Point
How to Not Crack Under Stress
Tough Love
Create a Strategy
Choose Every Battle
Have High Standards
When to Amputate
Normal Stages of Grieving

Chapter Eight: 8 Tips for Dealing with Other People's Problems
Tip #1: Fly in "V" Formation
Tip #2: Set Limits and Boundaries
Tip #3: Seek First to Empathize
Tip #4: Use Your Words Wisely
Tip #5: Stop Apologizing
Tip #6: Talk Back to Your Inner Critic, Shame and Guilt
Tip #7: Remain Calm and Think Before You React
Tip #8: How to Handle Resistance
The Four Magical Words to Deal with Resistance

Chapter Nine: Creating Authentic Power
Turn "Learned Helplessness" into "Learned Empowerment"
Your 10 Signature Strengths
How to Be Compassionate Yet Detached
Spiritual Empowerment
Peace of Mind and Stillness of Heart
Lessons from a Butterfly
Forgiveness

Chapter Ten: How to Let Go and Let God
Letting Go of Control
We Are All One Yet Separate

Chapter Eleven: Creating Space for Your Own Best Life
Self-Focus
What Oprah Knows for Sure
Finding Your Purpose
Hope Is a Thing With Feathers
Be Filled Up With Yourself
Positive Affirmations are Your Magic Words
Spiritual Practice
Let It Go
Comes the Dawn
Roar

Introduction: How I Stopped Being a Whipping Post

Open yourself up to a brilliant new way of living!
---Oprah Winfrey

How I Stopped Being a Whipping Post

Ever since I can remember, people with problems were magnetized to me like a moth to a flame. I began receiving positive validation for being "so helpful." I was compliant, nice, people-pleasing, accommodating, and easy to get along with. I could read people well and sensed when something was wrong. I became a master intuitive. I was an empathic listener and people always told me I was gentle, loving, warm and caring. I started forming my identity this way. I was the "resident expert" in reading the body language of others, dancing around others, and changing my colors like a chameleon. I was the "whipping post" for people with problems to dump on. It took a long time for me to realize I was the victim of OP (Other People) and OPP's (Other People's Problems).

When it came time to choose a career, I naturally decided on the "helping professions." I started out as a Criminology major, then changed to Education. I taught junior and senior high school for 10 years, then got my Master's Degree and Doctorate Degree in Counseling/Psychology. I became a Licensed Marriage and Family Therapist, and now a Professional Coach and Consultant. People with problems continued to be all around me. All my boyfriends had problems, all my friends had problems, my husband, my adult daughter, my family, my clients – they all had problems that I thought I could "fix." I finally shut my phone off at night while I slept, but then they started ringing my doorbell at all hours of the night. If I didn't answer the door they would bang on my windows. They would call me at work. They would stalk me.

This left very little time and energy for me to deal with my own problems. I was slowly becoming burned out and depressed. It wasn't until I started getting trained as a Coach that I started thinking about my own life and my own importance. The instructors asked us to write down our goals and dreams. I realized that I could clearly articulate my goals and wishes for everyone but myself. I could fill ten pages about how my daughter could become successful. I could talk endlessly about what was best for all my friends. I had a solid plan for helping my clients turn their lives around. But when it came to my own life I was filled with indecision and cloudy thinking. I defined my life by how other people around me were doing.

Then one day I had a breakthrough. A friend said to me, "You know Lyn, you could choose yourself first." I said, "Oh, I know, and I will, just as soon as I get this situation under control." She said, "Let's just try this out right now. What would your life look like once this situation got under control?" I described how happy I would be. She said, "Then be that way now. Just declare the situation under control. Done. Handled. Now focus on yourself." I explained why I couldn't do that since it was just "make believe." She said, "Oh, yeah? What if I told you that the situation will get handled just fine without your help?" Suddenly it dawned on me! I could back out of the problem and the solution and the problem would somehow, some way, someday, get resolved on its own! There was MY plan and there was God's plan. My plan didn't matter! I let go and sure enough, the problem got handled. And in a much better way than if I had intervened (interfered!). And, I got to have peace, joy, happiness and FUN!

Recovering People-Pleasers

Throughout this book I will use myself as an example, because I've had to overcome the need to attach to OPP's. I've had to learn how to detach in order to create my own best life. I've had to learn how to set limits and boundaries. I've had to become self-protective. I've had to become selfish. I've had to learn how to say "NO" and mean it. I've had to learn how to allow people to suffer their own natural consequences. It hasn't been an easy road, and I still keep learning every day. I still make mistakes and still have to recover. It will be a never-ending challenge for me due to the nature of my personality. I am what I call a "recovering people-pleaser."

I will mainly use my experience with my daughter, "Buffy, The Mother Slayer" as I call her, as an example. She is my only child and has been my most challenging "person with problems." Buffy is an adult now, living on her own with her own child. Our children are our greatest challenges when it comes to detachment. This book will focus on dealing with adult children, not minor children. We cannot detach as much from our minor children – we have to listen to their problems – we have to take care of them. This is the challenge we signed on for when we chose to have children. But once our children are adults, we can slowly work on the detachment and letting go process. We deserve to have a life <u>with and without</u> our children once they are grown. They deserve to have a life <u>with and without</u> us as well.

I will also use many other examples, as I feel they may be helpful to you. Whether your "problem people" are your children, family, friends, co-workers, clients, or acquaintances, they all need to be handled pretty much the same. I will tell you exactly HOW to detach. I will tell you exactly WHAT to do and say. It's up to you to start practicing. One baby step at a time, and you will eventually become BRAVE. You will find the COURAGE to be yourself and ask for what you want. You will find the STRENGTH to make confident declarations about how you will live, what you will tolerate, and what you won't.

I Just Want to Feel Good

Wayne Dyer, my personal Guru, has written umpteen books on self-help, personal growth and spirituality. What he has found after all his writing, research and contemplating is that our goal in life is *to feel good*. Wow, really? Just to feel good? Imagine, if you made this your goal – to feel good in all situations – how would your life change? After I read this, I made it a point to make sure I feel good every moment of every day. Anything that comes into my life that makes me feel bad either has to GO, or I have to get to work on fixing it, or I have to release it to my Higher Power. I love Dr. Dyer's outgoing message on his voice mail. "Hi, this is Dr. Dyer and I want to feel good. So if your message has to do with anything other than that, call Dr. Phil or Dr. Laura. Have a nice day."

I've learned to embrace every experience. Everything happens for a reason, for my highest good. It's all GOOD and it's all GOD. My new mantra is, "Nothing bad happens. It all happens for my and others' highest good." I've learned not to "play God" for myself or others. God has a plan for my life (and yours) and it is way better than any plan I could think up. I have desires of course, and when I pray and meditate I give these over to God and ask Him to take them. Then I can let go (and let God).

What Is Detachment?

I've heard of detachment, but until recently I didn't really know what it was or how to do it. I thought it was a bad thing, like ignoring people or not caring about people. I was taught from a young age to put other people before myself. I was taught to share, to listen, to care, to love, to give. This detachment thing sounded selfish and uncaring.

When I went to graduate school for my counseling degree my professors would always talk about being "empathic." It was the most important thing, they said, therapeutically, to look at someone in the eye, give them your total attention, and let them know you hear them and feel for them. That part was easy for me, since that's what I always did naturally.

In the 1970's a movement started called "encounter groups" which became very popular. Apparently people needed to learn how to have closer encounters with others, learn how to communicate better, and how to be more empathic. In the 1980's a movement started called "sensitivity training" which again, became very popular. This seemed to come out of the need to help people become more aware of and more tolerant of each other's differences. So for two decades people were being trained to be more sensitive to each other, which was extremely important for SOME people, and extremely detrimental for OTHERS.

I will explain more about this concept later, but it is important for you to know that everyone falls somewhere on a continuum from self-centered to other-centered. If you fall more on the "other-centered" side (like me), then you are probably at risk for being too sensitive to other people and their problems. At the extreme end of this side is what we call "highly sensitive people" (HSP). HSP are at risk for self-destructive behaviors as well as being abused by others. This book is for people who find themselves on the front end of the continuum. The continuum goes something like this:

Overly emotional and reactive, hysterical
Highly sensitive, often distressed

Controlling and/or manipulative
Overly worried, consumed with problems
Overly concerned
Concerned with emotion
Concerned with little emotion
Detachment with empathy
Interested
Unconcerned
Insensitive
In denial, shut down
Withdrawn
Self-centered
Self-absorbed
Narcissistic
Sociopathic

Highly Sensitive People

This book is geared toward those in the first half of this continuum. Sensitivity training is designed mainly for those in the second half of this continuum. So this means that half the people being trained in sensitivity are already way too sensitive, and the sensitivity training could put them over the edge. This may have resulted in the next huge movement in the 1980's called "co-dependency recovery." Co-dependency Anonymous (CODA) groups started up in every city in the U.S. Thankfully, there was finally a movement for people on the more sensitive side of the scale. Sensitivity to others' needs (over my own) was hammered into me by my culture, church, school, home, family, and employers. I really only knew how to be empathetic, caring, warm and unconditionally loving and giving, and I was good at it. I had no idea I was at HUGE risk for being taken advantage of and/or abused. Which is exactly what has happened. It was up to ME to find ways to "unteach" myself what had been ingrained in me. I found help through CODA and Al-Anon, which are based on the 12-Step Programs, counseling, support groups, assertiveness training, empowerment training, college professors, and great role models.

Along with the 12-Step Program boom came assertiveness training, leadership training, personal coaching and personal empowerment movements. More recently, there has been a strong movement toward "spiritual enlightenment" and "spiritual empowerment." The spiritual empowerment movement has helped me the most with detachment. It is based on knowing your inner soul, or God, or Higher Power, whatever you perceive that to be. It is about finding and following your "inner knowing." It is about building up the part of yourself that we call "intuition" or "gut instinct." It is also about building up your "chi." *Chi* is your life force or life energy – it's what keeps you moving forward and moving toward a better life.

Your "heart" is your emotion, and your nervous system, which is where anxiety comes from. In order to control anxiety you need to force yourself to move away from your emotions and nervous system to your head, where you can process things rationally. When you are a highly sensitive person, the goal is to lead with your head, then your gut, then your chi, and last, your heart. I will describe *desensitization* and how to do it.

I will be giving you dozens of ideas and strategies on how to emotionally detach from other people and their problems. Some of them will work for you, and some of them won't. There is no ONE right way to detach. Try as many of them as you feel comfortable with.

Don't follow any advice until you feel as deeply in your spirit as you think in your mind that the counsel is wise.
---Joan Rivers

Detached Concern

I had professors in my psychology curriculum who talked about the notion of "detached concern." They said the number one occupational risk for people in the helping professions was getting bogged down emotionally from taking on OPP's and becoming depressed. They said we needed to protect ourselves from carrying all our clients' problems on our backs. But they failed one very important part of our education. They didn't tell us HOW to do this. There were no books on the subject. When I asked, they all said they couldn't explain it. They told us how important empathy was – in fact it is the empathic attitude of the therapist that is the crux of all healing. But how do you have genuine empathic concern for someone while remaining detached emotionally? Do you have to become a Buddhist Monk?

In this book I'm going to tell you HOW. I will tell you <u>how to have compassion and detachment at the same time</u>. I will give you the exact thoughts to have running through your head. I will tell you the exact words to say. I'm not going to be like all the other authors who say "detach" but don't tell you *how*. I'm going to define this word for you and teach you how to do it until it is cemented in every cell of your body.

It's Not Easy – But Worth the Work

One thing I know for sure. I know what DOESN'T work. Abraham Maslow once said, "If all you have is a hammer, you see every problem as a nail." Once upon a time, I only had a hammer (my co-dependency and need to please, help, fix). Therefore every problem was a nail (one that required my "hammer"). I now have new tools for dealing with people and problems – and I want to share them with you. I now attract people who are high functioning rather than a hot mess. I'll share every good thing I know with you. But you'll need to do your part – not just reading, but ACTING. It's going to take some work. It's not going to be easy. It's going to feel awkward, unnatural, and inauthentic at times. You will need to rehearse, practice, and act "as if" a lot. People are going to resist the new you. People may even get mad at you. They will try to pull you back into your old role. You will feel uncomfortable for a while. It will often feel like a roller coaster ride. But take it from me, it will be the BEST thing you've EVER done for yourself! I promise it will be worth it!

Of all the 35 books I've written, this one has been by far the most difficult. It is the "deepest" book I've written. I had to dig much deeper into my mind, heart and soul to write this, and at times it brought up pain for me. I believe we teach best what we most need to learn, and man did I need to learn this! The most interesting thing that happened to me while writing this book was that I got "tested" every day. Every single time I sat down to write, I would get a phone call or text from someone who said they needed me. OP and OPP's were coming out of the woodwork! People I hadn't talked to in months or years began contacting me. I was able to practice all my new ideas dozens of times, and as we know, practice makes perfect! I'm certainly not perfect yet, but I'm a LOT better than I was, and I feel so much better, so much more of the time. I *needed* to write this book for myself as well as anyone else who is struggling with OPP's (which is just about everyone!).

By the time you've finished reading this book you will also have had some amazing breakthroughs. Yet here's the thing about breakthroughs. They are preceded by a feeling of uneasiness and/or distress. As they near, you may feel like there is no way out except the "old" way. There will be tremendous internal and external pressure to revert back to your old ways. The subconscious mind pulls you back to what is familiar. The subconscious mind equates familiarity with safety. You will need to hold tight to your breakthroughs. Changes feel uncomfortable until they take hold. But don't worry, you'll be fine. In fact the outcome will be better than you imagined. And when you see the result, you'll feel exhilarated!

My goal for you is that when you have finished this book, you will be able to rationally detach in any situation. You will be able to move freely in and out of your emotions and feelings. You will be able to replace negative thoughts and feelings with positive ones. You will be able to respond in the best way to any situation for everyone's highest good. You will be in control of your thoughts and emotions. You will feel good instead of bad. You will be able to summons your "inner knowing" any time you want. You will become a spiritual warrior. You will be who you are and say who you are. You will be strong, clear, empowered, and people will respect you. You will take your focus off OP and OPP's and place it where it belongs – on YOU.

Are you ready to take a brilliant leap forward? Are you ready to create space for your own best life? Are you ready to shift your perspective in order to set up a chain of reaction for your highest good? Are you ready to put yourself first? Well then, buckle up and get ready for the best ride of your life!

Be the heroine of your life, not the victim.
---Nora Ephron

Chapter One: It's Not Them, It's YOU

How to Protect Yourself from OPP's

Most of us assume our pain is the result of what someone else does or does not do. This is a form of self-victimization and it will keep you stuck in a muddy quagmire. This turns into quicksand, and will eventually drag you down and suffocate you. You MUST get out of this type of thinking! You must take full responsibility for how you are feeling. No one can control your feelings except you.

Other people have the power to "activate" feelings within you, but you do not have to give them a chair to sit on. When people come to you with their problems, your natural inclination is to want to help solve the problems. Your "reactive mind" kicks in and you feel a pain in your gut. Part of being human is to feel something for other human beings, and want to improve our world. Until you choose not to be controlled by these dynamics, you will feel that you have been "hurt" by other people, just as you will continue to feel that you have been hurt by other people in the past.

Even if you change the circumstances and people in your life who appear to be causing your pain, that pain will recur: the pain of abandonment, the pain of betrayal, the pain of letting go of an important relationship, or being abused or being judged. Further, when you look back on your experiences, you will see that already this pain has recurred many times in different situations, different places and with different people. Eventually you will see that YOU are the common denominator. You are the thread that connects. Judging others, blaming others, trying to punish others and gossiping about others will not ease your pain or prevent it from returning, because your pain is not caused by others. It occurs only when the dynamic is activated within you.

The good news is that each time the dynamic (your pain) is activated, for example, anger, abandonment, humiliation, you will have another opportunity to look inside. You will again feel the magnetic attraction of fear, the powerful pull of judgment, the need to prove that another person is causing your pain. But you can choose to experience the interior source of your pain—instead of blaming it on others.

Every time you break your usual pattern, you melt the wall between you and others, and can connect from an open heart. Eventually, you will recognize that each of your emotions is a free-standing experience, independent of what others do or say—and that the activation and reactivation of painful dynamics <u>will end when you intervene consciously in this process</u>. You will recognize the difference between "reacting" and "responding."

This is the first step to creating *authentic power*. When you think others are doing something to "hurt you," it is simply an illusion. It is based on your past trigger points of pain. Once you bring this to your conscious, it will no longer have power over you. The goal is to have power over your own thoughts and emotions, and not allow others to control your thoughts or feelings. Every time you feel that pain in your gut, stop and say to yourself, "This is not about him/her, it is about me, and I can control it."

This being said, there are people who actually do want to hurt you for whatever reason, be it jealousy, anger, revenge, etc. When I've noticed someone has said something hurtful to me or about me, I simply say, "Wow, that hurt," or "Ouch." Then I am quiet. Usually the person will apologize or explain it in a different way. I accept their apology, then I try to see if there is an element of truth in what they have said. If there is, I work to correct it. If there isn't, I let it go, and protect myself from this person in the future.

At this point in my life I'm very self-assured about what I want and where I'm going. I have this quote in my diary that I stick to: 'I do not intend to tiptoe through life only to arrive safely at death.'
---Christina Aguilera

What's Really Wiping Out All Your Energy?

I think you already know the answer to this question. Yes, you are right. It's OPP's. You take it all on – soak it up like a sponge. People are a constant interruption in your life. You just get started on a project you've been wanting to do for a long time. Then the phone rings. Yes, someone needs you NOW. So you drop everything and help them out. You somehow think that helping, worrying, talking, fretting, stressing, etc. will make it all better, but it won't. All it does is cause you to be tired, irritable, annoyed, angry and depleted.

I myself, am sick of people interrupting and interfering with my life and my goals. I now make it a point to shut off my cell phone when I'm working and concentrating on a project. I shut off my phone when I go to sleep at night. If there's an emergency they can call 911 instead of me! Seriously, what am I going to do to help anyone at 3am? It will only cause me to be overtired the next day and not able to deal with anything positively. I'm not the police, I'm not a paramedic, I'm not a nurse or a doctor or a hospital. If someone I love has an emergency there are plenty of other more capable people than me to help them. I can't tell you how many times my daughter has called me with an "emergency" only to find out it was some minor thing that was a result of her forgetfulness, laziness, or mismanagement of her life. I tell her, "Poor planning on your part does not constitute an emergency on mine."

When I was a junior high school teacher I had seven classes a day with over 30 kids in each class. That would be over 210 kids to handle each day, besides other assignments like hall duty, door duty, before school and after school activities. I'm not sure if you know this, but kids age 12 – 14 are the most needy people on earth. They are adorable, and loving, and sweet and generous and kind. Yet they are <u>the most attention-seeking people in the world</u>. When they love you, they just want to be with you. They want your attention – all of them – at once! I loved my students, but soon after I started teaching, I noticed I was exhausted at the end of the day. When I got home, all I could do was take a nap. They had sucked all the energy out of me. This was fine, until I had a child of my own, and could no longer take a nap after work. Now I had a baby who wanted all my attention for the next four hours, and a husband who wanted dinner and some quality time with me. I had nothing left to give. Again, I had reached my breaking point, and something had to give.

If One More Person Tells Me They Need Me I Will Scream!

"Ms. Kelley!" "Mom!" "Lyn!" "Watch me!" "Come see!" "Help me!" "I need (whatever)!" "Where is the (whatever)?" If I heard any of these words one more time I was going to scream and maybe even have a nervous breakdown. Everyone was pulling at my skirt, pants, and sleeves. I had no break, no rest, no "me" time. I determined I could not live this way any longer. I took a leave of absence from my job (which we could NOT afford!). I got a part time teaching job so that I could take a nap before picking up my daughter from the sitter. I declared that this was what I needed and everyone else was just going to have to deal with it. And guess what? They did! And it worked – and I was a better person for everyone else besides myself.

What I do now to protect myself and my time is make appointments with myself. I plan my day in advance and actually write each thing I plan to do that day on my calendar, with appointment times. This way, if someone asks for something I can say, "I have an appointment from 2:00 to 4:00," or, "I'm free from 4:00 to 5:00." I treat my appointments (plans) as important as doctor appointments. I don't need to tell people what my appointments are for. That's my business. They just need to know I'm busy – I already have plans.

If Mama ain't happy, ain't nobody happy.
    ---Oprah Winfrey

Chapter Two: The Seven Toxic People in Your Life

Sell crazy someplace else. We're all stocked up here.
---Line by Jack Nicholson in the movie *As Good As It Gets*

    Have you ever walked into a situation with a person who you thought you were on good terms with, only to criticized, bashed, made wrong, demeaned, degraded, disrespected or unfairly treated? It can feel like you just got hit with a Mack truck. Right in the middle of your stomach. It sometimes just comes out of nowhere so you had no time to prepare for battle. You are so shocked and confused that you are thrown completely off balance. You've been blind-sided. You don't know what to do or say. You can't believe what you are hearing. The fight or flight syndrome hits and you either want to run away or fight back.
    Sometimes the abuse doesn't come on suddenly, but after you've been hanging out with someone for a while and the conversation begins to change for the worse. Sometimes it happens after people have been drinking alcohol. Sometimes it's a "hit-and-run." Sometimes it is so subtle that we don't realize we've been hit until later. Sometimes we leave feeling "beat up" and don't know why. Well, I'm here to tell you that you are not going to get beat up, disrespected or bullied <u>any more</u>. You are going to be prepared, and you will know what to do the *nano-second* someone starts throwing shade on you.

Baiters

    According to Dr. Phil, we all have at least one "B.A.I.T.E.R" in our life. These are the Backstabbers, Abusers, Imposters, Takers, Exploiters and Reckless people who Dr. Phil says could be <u>taking advantage of you</u>. If you are a nice person, who genuinely cares about people, you are bound to have some baiters in your life. People sense your niceness and will take advantage of it if you let them. They find your weaknesses, your emotional buttons, and proceed to press them over and over. They will jerk you around, lift you up and tear you down, degrade you, damage you, and leave you for dead. They don't care about you. They only care about what you can do for them and if you don't do it exactly the way they want you to they turn on you.

You need to rid your life of these unsavory characters intent on tearing you down. But more importantly, you need to change the way you react and respond to them so they will know right off the bat that you are NOT to be reckoned with. They need to know you mean business, and you intend to have a reciprocal relationship. You must teach people how to treat you. I'll explain more about that later. I've created a tag line for myself: "I may be blond, but I'm smart. I may be tiny but I'm mighty. I may be nice, but push me too hard and "nice" is not what you'll remember about me. Don't underestimate me." I don't say this out loud, but think it to myself. It helps me get through difficult times with difficult people. I hope you'll create a tag line of your own!

You need to protect yourself from people who take undue advantage and suck the energy out of your life. They rob you of your peace. They rob you of your "chi" (your life force). I call these people "chi vampires" or "emotional vampires."

See Dr. Phil's video *How to Rid Yourself of Toxic Relationships* here: http://www.oprah.com/oprahshow/Dr-Phil-How-to-Let-Go-of-Toxic-Relationships-Video

Haters

Haters are basically people who are critical of you and make you wrong. They don't come to you and ask permission to talk to you about something that is bothering them in order to improve the relationship. They don't come in a respectful way or a loving way or with a kind spirit. They come with jealousy, envy, resentment, pain, fear, anger, and sometimes with downright meanness. Celebrities have the most haters because of several reasons. First, they usually try to connect with their "fans" through social media outlets, websites, blogs, and public appearances. They put themselves out there for people to get to know, which often sets them up for criticism. Second, they usually try to allow their "fans" to get to know them by having conversations via social media, blogs and emails. This way non-celebrities feel like they "know" them and therefore they think this somehow this gives them the right to talk to them any way they want. Third, people are most jealous and envious of celebrities, especially when they are unhappy with their own lives.

And fourth, celebrity gossip (bashing) has become a mainstream part of the media, so it gives people "permission" to do the same.

Imagine how important it is then, for celebrities to learn how to detach from all the negative press. They receive hate mail, hate email, hate social media postings, hate articles in tabloids, hate comments on celebrity talk shows, often on a daily basis. They have to de-sensitize themselves from the hate. They have to work extra hard on keeping their self-esteem in tact. They have to be able to let it go, whether the hate talk is true or untrue (and I'm imagining it's much more difficult to deal with when the hate talk is untrue!). They have to go on to their next gig and be at their best for their *real* fans. As they say, "The show must go on." If they can do it, the rest of us "average" people can too. Even one of the most popular and most loved women in the music industry, Taylor Swift, wrote a song about haters called, *Shake it Off*.

In his book, *Act Like a Success, Think Like a Success*, comedian and talk show host Steve Harvey outlines the different categories of haters to be on the look-out for. These are, the "I hate everything hater," the "drag you down hater, the "situational hater," and the "self-hate hater." He tells Oprah on her *Lifeclass* show that haters are most hurtful when they are related to you, but whether they are friends, acquaintances, relatives, co-workers, or strangers, they basically need to be handled the same way. He says, "You can't tell big dreams to small-minded people. You may have a person in your life that you can no longer take on your journey. You can't progress when you have haters around you." As Joel Osteen says, "Love them from a distance."

Emotional Vampires

Emotional Vampires are the people in your life that constantly need something from you. They confound you, confuse you, and seem to sap every ounce of your energy. They may be spouses, lovers, relatives, friends, and children. I had a friend who was totally an emotional vampire. She seemed high functioning and well managed. She started calling me every day talking to me about all of her problems with friends, lovers, family, and co-workers. Somewhere around our 21st or 22nd vent session, I realized that we were just rehashing the same old things. She wasn't interested in improving things, it turns out; she just really liked crying and complaining. The more I got stuck in her cycle, the more trapped I felt. All of my energy was consumed by my frustration that she just wanted to complain and would never accept any constructive advice. I felt used and taken advantage of. Sometimes I felt like asking her, "What do you want from me, my BLOOD? Do you want me to POP a VEIN???" This is when I knew she was a vampire, and I had allowed her to suck my blood dry. I finally had to let her go. Later, I will tell you how to let go of emotional vampires.

Controllers

Another friend wanted to be MY personal coach and trainer. Every morning she filled up my email inbox and Facebook feed about all her accolades – her 3.7 mile jog at 5:00am, her motivational quotes of the day and her healthy, gluten-free breakfast. At lunchtime she would Instagram a "fitsperation" photo of her progress on *CrossFit* and tag me in a Facebook post about an underwater kickboxing class I should try. At first I felt she was really motivating and positive, but after a while I started feeling under fire. She was so interested in living healthy that she was always telling me what I should eat and not eat, grilling me on my workout routine, and showing me how I could fit more into my schedule each day. That motivation – though well-intentioned, led me into a shame spiral. I realized she was somewhat of a fanatic (neurotic?) so I finally had to back off. I still saw her once in a while, but made sure it was while exercising so I could allow her to motivate me without getting bogged down by her.

Look, we all have weaknesses and our self-esteem is fragile. We don't have the "luxury" of a negative thought. Only allow yourself to spend time with people who are validating, supportive and encouraging. Now, when I notice that "irk" in my gut, I realize I need to protect myself. I need to go straight to my brain and decide whether I need to stand up and say something, or listen without reaction, or release them to my Higher Power, or get away as fast as I can (or a combination of these!).

We all want to feel in control, at least in control of ourselves. Everyone is controlling sometimes. While reading this book you might discover you've been dealing with controlling, manipulative behaviors from other people in your life – your boss, parent, child, friend, mate, or other person. You may have experienced being "bullied" in your childhood, and may still be being emotionally bullied. This book will help you learn how to deal with ALL controlling and bullying people more effectively.

People range on a continuum from extremely controlling (to the point of manipulation and/or criminal behaviors) to extremely passive (to the point of being a sickly, weak doormat). As you can see, both ends of the continuum are very unhealthy and destructive. Finding a happy medium is not an easy task. Some of us were lucky enough to have great role models in our families of origin and throughout our formative years, so getting to a healthy place is much easier. Unfortunately, most of us did not have this benefit, and we have to find our way through the ups and downs of adult relationships (experiencing pain and distress along the way!).

As difficult and painful as it is to find a place of "healthy control" in relationships, it seems we are quite motivated to keep trying. Our innate need for interpersonal relationships (connecting with others) must be very high, otherwise most of us would become hermits. People who try to control others usually feel insecure within themselves, and even more insecure within the relationship. Controlling people tend to seek out passive and compliant people. The reason for this is to "even the scale." We are genetically programmed to want "equality" and fairness, and we subconsciously feel we need to respond by either over controlling or under controlling. So when you feel you are being controlled or dominated, you will either give in and give people what they want, or you will become controlling as well. Both responses are unhealthy.

This is why I love the 12 Step Program. The first step is: "We admitted we were powerless over (fill in the blank.) First we need to admit that we have no power of others. The second step is: "We came to believe that a power greater than ourselves could restore us to sanity." <u>God's power gives us personal power</u>. But this power is meant for us, for our own lives, to focus on what we want and need for ourselves.

If you determine that you do indeed have some overly compliant or overly controlling tendencies, you'll need to take care of yourself first. You cannot change another person, you can only change yourself. Once you change, the other person automatically changes in response. The goal is to detach from the situation emotionally. Do not react. Take some time to think about what is going on with the other person and what is going on inside of you. Remind yourself not to give in or fight, but seek something in between. Often it is helpful to first ask the other person <u>what it is they want from you</u>. This is a very powerful question. Ask them to be very specific. Keep asking until you are sure you understand. Keep asking until you are sure the other person is sure. If need be, don't respond right away. Ask for some time to think about it. You may find this ONE THING will change your relationship dramatically for the better.

    Many people have a passive personality and don't stand up for themselves. They have weak personal boundaries because they have low self-esteem. They simply do not feel they are worthy of saying who they are and asking for what they want. Many people don't even know who they are because they've been too busy being a chameleon to fit whatever everyone else wants them to be. If you find you have been weak, passive and compliant in many of your significant relationships, you will need to take the first step of working on getting stronger within yourself. I have had to work on this my entire life!

    The most important skill anyone can learn is good communication skills. Learning who you are, saying who you are, saying what you want, and saying it in the right way, at the right time, with the right amount of intensity, are critical skills to have in any relationship. Oprah has said she believes her "gift" is her "voice." I would go further than that, and say her "gift" is "speaking her truth." The way she asks questions, listens with empathy, offers positive regard, and says how she feels, is truly amazing. She can be filled with emotion for someone or something, and even cry openly, yet she doesn't seem to get stuck there. She can move in and out of her various emotional spaces freely and at will. She has been one of my greatest role models in communication.

    Ask your close friends and relatives if they ever see you as too passive or too controlling. Ask them to rate you on a scale from one to ten – one being very passive, five being healthy assertive, and ten being very controlling/manipulative. I have actually been attracted to controlling men my whole life, and many of them have told me their biggest complaint about me was that I was too "nice" and too "passive." Don't worry, I don't get that anymore!

Life is hard enough as it is without choosing someone difficult to share it with.
---Greg Behrendt

Manipulators

Manipulative people are always controlling, but controlling people aren't necessarily manipulative. Manipulation is a more severe form of controlling, so if you are with a controlling person you need to know what signs to look out for. I call controlling manipulators CM's. Being with a controlling person is often distressing, but being with a manipulative person is crazy-making. There are many types of controlling behavior, most of which can be dealt with by a strong, self-assured, assertive response. Manipulation is much more difficult to deal with because it is often covert and outside of our awareness. When we're being manipulated we always have a feeling that something isn't right, but usually can't pinpoint exactly what it is. This is called *emotional manipulation*.

Emotional manipulators are about covert control. These types of people are the most intelligent, usually geniuses. They have learned how to manipulate people through their emotions, and most victims get so caught up in the emotional part that they completely lose their rational thought. So even the most intelligent of people can get sucked down their rat hole.

Emotional manipulators are like crack dealers. They provide huge doses of fun, compliments, adoration, good manners, affection, gifts and delights (drugs) in the beginning of a relationship. Then, once you're hooked, the drugs get shorter in supply and more expensive. They expect much more from you in return for their drugs. They may even expect you to be their idea of "perfect." If you fall short in any way, they will take away the drug completely, or threaten to. They control you through what psychologists call "behavior modification." They begin to give you the drug only intermittently, and only when you are "good." They may use withdrawal, criticism, or scare tactics to get you to behave the way they want you to. They know how to push all your emotional buttons to get you down. And "down" is where they want you. You must be "below" them. They must emotionally weaken you in order to keep you in the "one down" position. When you are down, you are much more easily manipulated.

You need to be aware of how and when you are being manipulated. Emotional manipulators' main tactics are guilt-tripping, criticizing and shaming. Manipulators know that most people have a different kind of conscience than they do. They are often skilled at using this as a means of keeping their victims in a self-doubting, anxious, and submissive position. The more conscientious the victim, the more guilt is an effective weapon. All a manipulator has to do is suggest that you don't care enough, are too selfish, etc. and you immediately start to feel bad and weaken.

Shaming is a subtle technique of using sarcasm and put-downs as a means of causing you to feel fear and self-doubt. If they can get you to feel inadequate, you will be the weaker party, thereby maintaining their position of dominance. When you notice someone is using one of these tactics, you need to confront it directly. Name it for what it is. Say, "This feels like emotional manipulation. You cannot control me by guilt-tripping. Tell me what it is you want from me and I will determine whether or not I can work with you."

Moochers

Moochers are people who take advantage of us. They range from those who are constantly asking to borrow money to those who expect us to take care of them and pay for all their needs and desires without giving anything in return. A healthy relationship involves give and take. Sometimes you will be giving more and sometimes he/she will be giving more. If you feel you are giving more than you are receiving most of the time, you probably are. You need to trust your gut instincts on this so you don't get "taken" for a joyride.

Here's an example of a typical "moocher" type. You meet a very nice, attractive artist who seems to just be "down on his luck." He is sweet, sensitive, affectionate – different from most men. He does just enough for you (compliments, gestures, positive attention) to make you think he is deep down a good, kind person. You are attracted to him physically and see that he has lots of potential. He is very intelligent, gifted and talented. He complains that he loves his "work," but he just hasn't gotten the "break" he needs to really take off with it. You admire his passion. If only you could help him get his break.

Okay, now you're going into fantasyland. You are his rescuer – you can give him what no woman ever has – you can help him be successful! Once he is achieving success he will be so grateful and so appreciative that he will put you up on a pedestal, treat you like a princess, and of course – NEVER leave you. HE is the "damsel in distress" and YOU are his "knight in shining armor." Yes, I know, the storybooks told the story in reverse, but nevertheless, you WANT to help him. You are now so passionate about him that you NEED to help him. You are obsessed with helping him and NOTHING will get in your way!

He's a starving artist and you become his provider. And what are you asking in return? Well, of course, you're hoping the story will play out like the fairy tales and he will fall in love with you, marry you, and you will live happily ever after. Also, there are some ways you see he could help you. After all, he's good at fixing things around the house, he can lift heavy things, he loves to cook, he is great in bed, and he is so good looking, well-groomed and stylishly dressed that he sure makes you look good in public. He makes your social status go way up. Besides, he's a man and he will protect you, stand by you, take care of you and love you! That's all the payoff you need. Or so you think.

Above all you must not get sucked into "fantasy thinking." You must look at the situation for what it is. You must attempt to create a fair and reciprocal relationship right from the start rather than "hoping" this person will repay you down the road. When my daughter asks me for ANYTHING now, I always stop before I say yes, and think of what I want in return from her. I insist on reciprocal relationships. I will ask her to commit to giving me what I want – sometimes I even make her sign a contract. Hey, as Donald Trump says, "Nothing personal. It's just business." <u>And you must be in the business of self-protection every minute of every day</u>!

Drama Addicts

Many people are addicted to emotional drama. Many people grew up in homes that were so chaotic, so emotionally charged, so drama-filled, that this is how they "learn" to live. Unless their hearts are pounding, they're sweating with anxiety and thrown off balance inconsistently, in the throes of passion and pain, they can't stand it. Emotional stability feels boring. This problem can be serious, causing illness and depression. People who are addicted to emotional drama will create it if it isn't already there. But here's the kicker. They don't want to be alone in their drama. They need to suck other people in to it. They feel important when they are able to get other people to listen, get caught up with them emotionally, and get upset alongside them.

It's sort of like the "Type T" personality. Type T is a thrill seeker. Some people are addicted to thrilling activities such as rollercoasters, bungee jumping, hang gliding, sky diving, etc. They may also love seeing fear invoking movies with horror, violence, murder, destruction and gore. I've never been a thrill seeker, but it seems thrill seekers seek me out. I could never understand why a thrill seeker would want to be with a quiet, stable, dependable person. But if finally dawned on me – they need someone to help stabilize them. They know they can go too far and get out of control and even scare themselves.

I've had more drama addicts as friends than I can count. Again, they are magnetized to people who are sensitive, caring, loving, and sympathetic. If you feel you are on an emotional roller coaster with a person, it's time to either get out or get counseling. If you often feel upset, angry, confused, helpless, sad, or desperate, please know that this is NOT what a relationship should be about. While we all have some of these feelings some of the time, feeling them a lot of the time is <u>not good for you</u>. It's not fair for someone to dump all their "crazy" onto you. It's not a reciprocal relationship. They are using you and taking advantage of you. You cannot afford to get bogged down continually by another person's drama. They need to get professional help. <u>Period.</u>

Recently I became closer friends with someone who previously more of an acquaintance. At first, she seemed normal. She seemed high functioning, stable, had a good job, intelligent, spiritual, and well rounded. Soon she began calling me for advice with problems. The problems she was having seemed odd considering what I had previously thought of her. Then the problems started escalating. When I asked her if she had taken my previous advice to ward off the problems, she admitted that she hadn't, and couldn't for fear of repercussions. She was caught in a bind. She wasn't able to receive good advice because she was staunchly attached to keeping the emotional drama in her life. When I finally realized there was nothing I could do to help her, I told her in the most loving way I possibly could that I cared about her but I was getting too overloaded and brought down by her problems. I felt I was not able to help and offered to help her find a good therapist. She said she didn't feel she needed a therapist. So I began easing my way out of the friendship as tactfully as I could.

When reading this book, if you notice that you have a tendency to attract emotional drama addicts, I encourage you to follow my advice and protect yourself.

The 10 Best Ways to Manage Toxic People

There are several ways to deal with a controlling and/or manipulative person (CM). I recommend you try all of the strategies I give you, and see which one(s) work the best. Maybe you'll find that at certain times, one or another will work better, so it's good to have several strategies prepared in advance, to use when needed. With CM's you'll need to be armed. You'll need to be aware. You'll need to be ready with your arsenal of weapons and protective gear. This is the only way to handle them before things get out of control. Here are some behaviors you can try.

Never try to teach a pig to sing. It doesn't work and will just annoy the pig.
---Anonymous

One: Be aware of the problem

Awareness is the first step – you need to get out of your own denial. He/she probably is unaware of the problem as well. He/she needs YOU to explain it to him/her. At first you may only be able to "see" the problem after it has happened. That's ok, you can always bring up the issue at a later time. As you catch on to how you're feeling when someone is behaving in a controlling or manipulative way, you will be able to pinpoint the behavior as it is happening so that you can confront it on the spot. So the first step is not to REACT. The first step is to stop and become aware. Be aware of what this person is communicating. Be aware of how you are feeling. Be aware of what your reactive impulse would be, but don't do it. Just breathe.

Eckert Tolle, the great spiritual guru, says that when a person comes to him with a problem, he simply says, "Is that so?" This is a non-emotional response which implies interest. It also is putting the problem back onto the communicator. It is asking a question, which causes the person to have to elaborate more. Once they have elaborated more, Tolle says, "Is that so?" This actually causes the other person to keep talking until they may actually start to work out their own solutions.

Two: State the problem and allow them to solve it

Who you are is much more important than what you say. Show up as someone who is on your friend's side. You are completely, 100% there for him/her. They have your undivided attention, and let me tell you, this is a rarity in today's world! People pay therapists $150 an hour just to have someone fully listen to them, without judgment. You can be this type of friend. In fact, this is the most therapeutic thing you can do in any situation. Having someone by your side that communicates "I am here for you" is the most important thing you can do for anyone.

When someone knows you are there for them, and are on their side, they will continue to open up to you. When you align yourself with them and let them know you understand their fears and frustrations, they may be much more open to you. This way they will trust you enough to talk to you and share their deeper thoughts. Notice I did not say, "This way they will trust you enough to tell you more." Your goal is not for them to tell you more about their problem. Your goal is for them to solve their problem themselves, without any help, advice, or guidance from you. Once they see that you are a caring, empathic listener, they will kept talking about their problem until they have come up with their own solutions.

Oprah Winfrey became the most watched talk show host in the world within one year of her show. She went on to become a multi-billionaire with her own television network. How did this happen? She came from poverty, she was a minority in a white man's world, she wasn't particularly beautiful or educated according to Western society. She did this by being the first talk show host who asked questions and listened empathically. She didn't try to solve people's problems. She just listened and showed them that she completely understood. And this was all it took. We can learn a lot from this. Remember, as Tony Robbins says, "Success leaves clues."

Do not own the problem. The problem belongs to the other person. If you make him/her the problem he/she will be defensive. If you make yourself the problem, or make yourself the problem solver, you will lose your power. When you make the other person own the problem, he/she is forced to look at possible solutions. Say something like, "I can see that this is a great concern to you. What do you think you can do to make it better for you?" Notice I said the word "you" three times. You want to put the problem back onto them, so it is not in your lap. You are like the backboard. The ball bounces off you and goes right back to them.

Three: Make your feelings important

Feelings are not right or wrong, they just are. No one has the right to judge your feelings. If something is important to you, it should be important to the other person. If someone says you're overreacting, simply restate your feelings and let them know they need to take your feelings into account. They don't have to agree with your feelings, they don't have to feel your feelings, they just need to acknowledge that they are your feelings and that they matter, as do theirs. Obviously people respond better to feelings when they are expressed in a mature, rational manner. If you want others to take your feelings seriously, you need to express them in a rational manner. It may be necessary to rehearse your speech before you give it to them so you don't end up a weeping, pathetic mess.

Some people thing they must overly exaggerate their feelings in order for others to "hear" them. Men often resort to yelling and women often resort to whining and crying. It is NOT TRUE that you need to overly emote, and it is NOT TRUE that they will take you more seriously if you do. If someone doesn't take you seriously when you state your feelings in a calm, mature manner, <u>it shows they just don't take you seriously</u>. This now, becomes your <u>major issue</u>. You may find you are trying to talk to someone who really doesn't care about you or your feelings. It's hard to believe that someone WE care about may not care about US. But the reality is that, as I've stated, everyone falls somewhere on a continuum from self-centered to other-centered. If you find you are dealing with a self-centered, insensitive person, who doesn't take you seriously, you either need to ask them to make some changes or spend less time with them.

Four: Understand their Feelings Too

Ask the other person how he/she feels about the problem (and don't let him/her tell you there isn't a problem, because you know there is!). If they start becoming loud or controlling, they are clearly not in a mind frame to discuss it rationally at this time. Simply state, "I would like to have a rational, calm, two-way discussion about this and clearly you aren't up to it right now, so I will go ahead and leave and give you some time to process it. When you're ready to talk, let me know." Be very sweet and light about your departure. People often need time (much more time than we do) to know how they feel. They may not be as "in touch" with their feelings as we are, and frankly, our feelings may scare them. If they are scared it is likely they are going to be defensive, so give them all the time they need. Respecting their need for processing time is respecting their feelings. You should respect them in the same way you want them to respect you, right? If they do not come back within two or three days to discuss it, this is a sign that they are either shut down emotionally or really don't care.

Five: The "Shock and Awe" Strategy

If someone starts acting controlling or manipulative, you can simply ask a question that will most likely stop them in their tracks. Simply, ask "What???" By simply saying ONE WORD, asked as a question, with a perplexed look on your face, this person will automatically get that you don't understand what he/she is talking about. Your "what?" will take him/her off their position. You could say something like, "Excuse me???" or "Did you really just say that?" The important thing is to say it and then just stand there looking dumbfounded. This puts the onus on the other person. Now he/she will have to explain what he/she means. If the person starts changing the subject or diverting, simply say, "I don't understand." By acting "shocked" he/she will know they have done or said something you don't like, and will usually self-correct.

Another strategy is to simply look at the person and say, "Ouch." They will know they have hit a nerve with you. Say nothing else, and walk away. The person will eventually come around and apologize if they want to keep you in their lives.

Six: Absurdity

Another strategy that is similar to "shock and awe" is "absurdity." No one wants to feel they are being "absurd." Yet many times others' actions do feel absurd! When you notice they are acting or speaking in a way that is controlling, you could turn it into an absurdity by saying something like, "That's absurd." They may get angry or defensive, but at least you'll have given them the communication that this is not your reality of how life should be.

One time I had a controlling boyfriend who would constantly say things like, "You're not in the real world," or "You're an idealist." We went round and round arguing about what is a realist, an idealist, or an optimist. Of course, we all would rather be seen as realists and optimists, so I would try to convince him that this was what I was. After a few months of this, I realized he just wasn't going to "get it." And I finally learned that you should never have to *convince* people of who you are. They should be able to accept who you are. Once you get into the "convincer" role, you are in the weaker position. You simple tell them how you feel, what you think, and who you are. If they don't like it, so be it. You don't need to convince anyone – knowing who you are is enough!

Then next time he told me I was being an idealist, I said, "You know, it's been my experience that when someone becomes critical of another person, they are preparing to do something they will be ashamed of." Then I walked away. Yes, my statement was absurd! Sometimes you just have to <u>deal with absurdity with absurdity</u>. I've also responded with things like, "When you say things like that it makes my foot itch," and then I proceed to take off my shoe and itch my foot like crazy. Once I responded with, "Ouch, that hit my funny bone!" and proceeded to run around the house like a crazy person, as though I had just hit my funny bone and was in intense pain combined with uncontrollable laughter.

Once I told someone, "Dude, back off my grill!" which caused them to start laughing because who would have thought I knew hip-hop language? When my daughter comes to me with problems I often say, "Why are you taking me away from my happy place?" These ideas often work because they are a way of "diffusing" control tactics. They will cause the person to either be confused, dumbfounded, or amused. Either way, it takes all the pressure off the situation by diverting it, and reducing it to something rather silly, which of course, it is.

Seven: The "No-Contact" Strategy

Sometimes you need to be strong, in a nice, yet matter-of-fact way. You can't change another person. People only change when they are ready and want to change. You must simply state that this is who you are, this is what you want, and this is what you will and won't tolerate. Then you remove yourself from the situation and have no contact (or as little as possible) until the person comes around. The longer you stay "in discussion" or "in argument" or "in conflict" with this person, the more entrenched the problem will become. Walking away gives you much more power.

Often people don't respond to words, they only respond to NO CONTACT. The power of no contact is that when you withdraw, they consciously or subconsciously know why, and will most likely self-correct. They will most likely get into surrender mode after they miss you enough. If you find that this person responds better when you withdraw, you need to think about whether or not you want a relationship that requires so much distance. It it's a constant push-pull, what kind of relationship is that? I can understand if it only happens once in a while, like every few months or years, but if you find you are withdrawing often, you need to ask yourself if this is what you want for the rest of your life. This situation usually doesn't improve over time, it gets worse.

When the person is ready to discuss the problem in a calm, rational manner, tell him/her what you want. Be specific, such as, "I want you to be on time whenever possible, and if it is impossible, I want you to call me ahead of time and let me know. Can you do that?" Ask for commitment to change. Get a firm "yes" or "no" from him/her. Don't let the person use diversion tactics like waffling, skirting and dodging.

The person may want to negotiate some sort of compromising. I find most of us compromise ourselves far too much. Be careful you don't agree to something you'll regret later. If the compromise seems fair, go ahead. If you aren't sure, or something doesn't feel right about it, ask for a day or two to think about it. Don't compromise your strongest values or your integrity. The most important thing to remember about compromise is that it is a two-way street. Don't lose the "me!"

The best defenses are solid, emotional fences.
---Oprah

Eight: Pull Out of the Power Struggle

I love the term "strong surrender." All you have to do is three simple things: state the problem, what you would like to have done differently, and ask for an agreement. Then, physically lean back. Let the person respond. Listen and nod in understanding. Then restate what you want. Be a broken record if you need to be. Don't allow the person to pull you into a verbal conflict or change the subject. Your goal is to state your peace, then let the other person do the problem solving. Leaning back shows you are ready to receive. What you want to receive is the person's commitment to doing things differently. If the person still refuses to surrender (surrendering means accepting the problem and working through it to resolution in a calm, rational manner), go back to number four and offer to leave until the person is ready. Believe me, your absence will have more power than your presence in resolving this problem!

For example, a friend of mine was trying to call me but I had turned off my phone for an hour to take a rest and meditate. When I turned on my phone I had several ranting, raging messages from her asking why I don't answer my phone. I called her back and said, "Hey, I was taking a rest and turned off my phone. What's up?" She proceeded to go on and on about how angry she gets when I don't answer and asked why I turn off my phone. I simply said, "Why do you ask?" When she said she didn't understand why I do that, I simply asked, "What don't you understand?" She said she didn't understand why I can't just leave my phone on when I rest. I said, "Hmmm. You don't understand why a person wouldn't want to be disturbed during a rest, prayer or meditation time?" She said she did not. I said, "Okay, I guess we're just different in that way." Then I got back to the original subject, which was why she was calling me in the first place!

A smart eagle doesn't show her claws.
---Native American Saying

Nine: Regain Your Own Control

There are three entities in any relationship – *me*, *you* and *the relationship*. Focusing on the *third* entity (the relationship) is what makes it last. Focusing on the relationship is a very helpful detachment strategy, because it's not about YOU. It's a very helpful communication strategy because it's not about the OTHER PERSON either. Most people can agree on ONE thing, and that is that they would like a good relationship with each other. Getting to agreement on this ONE thing can start your communication on the right foot.

Usually we don't know how much power (control) we really have. We feel helpless when we're up against a very controlling person. Yet, we do not have to give away our control. Sometimes just saying something simple like, "No, I don't want that," or "That doesn't feel right to me" is enough to regain our power. Most of us have not been taught (and have not had adequate role models to show us) how to handle control and manipulation in healthy ways.

It's important to remember that people are basically lazy and self-centered in relationships. Especially when you allow them to be. People will only treat you the way you ALLOW them to treat you. You will only get that which you are willing to tolerate. You need to raise your expectations NOW and lower your tolerations NOW – before it's too late!

The most important aspects of relationships are trust and respect. We need to put these two qualities first. If we can't figure out how to trust and respect each other, the relationship is doomed. The three entities in the relationship are all equally important. If you lose the "me," the relationship will go downhill. The first and most important aspect in handling controlling people is YOUR SELF ESTEEM. You need to know yourself, like yourself, and feel free to express yourself. If you have had trouble with this aspect I suggest you get some coaching or counseling.

Men will not behave unless you have rules and standards.
---Steve Harvey

Ten: Offer Professional Help

Manipulation often comes in the more severe form of lying, cheating and stealing. Lying, cheating and stealing are signs of antisocial behavior and could become a severe personality disorder which we often call "sociopath" (the clinical term is antisocial personality disorder). This disorder is one of the most difficult ones to treat, as one of the main characteristics of the disorder is that the individual does not have a normal "conscience" and cannot see that their behavior is wrong, or has convinced themselves that they have done no wrong. The person does not feel guilt. Until a person can honestly admit they have a problem and ask for help, they will probably never change.

If you feel you are with a CM and you have tried dealing with him/her to no avail, you might want to find a good therapist who specializes in dealing with CM. Offer going to counseling with the person rather than telling them they need to see a therapist on their own. A good therapist will surely determine whether this person would benefit from seeing someone individually and can make that recommendation. It's much better when a person hears these things from a professional, rather than you.

Forcing a person into therapy with ultimatums usually do not work because CM's have already learned how to "con" people so well that they may seem cooperative on the outside while planning their "escape" on the inside. Inexperienced or untrained therapists can easily get manipulated by the CM, and it is very common to see a CM in therapy for years before the therapist gets that he/she has been completely bamboozled.

Nevertheless, if the relationship is important enough to you, you should never give up until you've at least attempted to get the person into some sort of professional assistance with you. This could be a mediator, a minister, a counselor, a coach, or a doctor. If the person refuses, it would still be helpful for you to see a professional until you feel you can detach from the situation emotionally.

How to Treat a Snakebite

Toxic people are like snakes. All snakes are dangerous, although only some snakes are poisonous. To prevent snakebites, you need to learn about snakes. It doesn't really matter if the snake is poisonous or not – you just need to stay away from them. Here are instructions on how to avoid snakebites, and what to do if you have been bitten. You can easily compare snakebites with difficult and toxic people in your life. And for sure, you need to stay away from snakes.

Understand the behavior of snakes. Snakes are "cold-blooded," meaning they get their body heat from their surroundings and the sun. Compare this to a person who is "hot" – angry, intoxicated, or upset.

Avoid contact with snakes. The best way to treat a snake bite is to avoid a snake bite. Don't sleep or rest next to areas where snakes may be hiding, this includes brush, tall grass, big rocks, and trees. Compare this to staying away from dangerous neighborhoods and/or situations.

Don't poke your hands into rock crevices, hollow logs, heavy brush, or any place a snake may be waiting for its next meal. Compare this to poking around in other people's business.

Look down as you walk through any brush or tall grass. Compare this to staying alert, aware and conscious of your situation and environment at all times.

Don't try to pick up any snake, dead or alive. Snakes have a reflex where they can bite for a minute or so after they are dead. Compare this to staying clear of potentially dangerous people – if you think they may need help, call 911 or ask someone for help.

ALWAYS wear hiking boots to cover your ankles and keep your pants legs tucked into your boots. Compare this to wearing your invisible coat of armor.

Make noise. Most snakes don't want to see you anymore than you want to see them! To ensure that you don't scare a snake, make sure they can hear you coming. Compare this to letting people know you are present and ready for any potential problem, while minding your own business.

Most snakes will not bite unless they are disturbed or handled by people. Compare this to not starting an argument or allowing a conflict to escalate with a difficult person. Walk away calmly and politely. Excuse yourself to the restroom if necessary, then plan your escape.

If you have been bitten by a snake, take these precautions. First, move away beyond striking distance of the snake. This means to get away as quickly as possible to a safe place. Second, lie down with the wound below the heart. This means to focus on your brain and your soul – to protect your heart (emotions). Third, keep still to avoid the venom from spreading. This means to stay calm and don't react right now. Fourth, cover the wound with a loose, sterile bandage. This means to take care of yourself by relaxing and staying as calm as possible. Fifth, call for help.

Here are the things you should NOT do if bitten by a snake. Do not cut a bite wound. Do not attempt to suck out venom. Do not drink alcohol or caffeinated drinks. Obviously, these things would make the situation worse. You may need an anti-venom treatment and/or tetanus shot. A tetanus shot is like getting a booster from a caring friend, a healthcare provider, therapist, clergy, CODA or Al-Anon meeting, or a life coach. Your goal is to protect your emotions and get back to your peaceful place as soon as possible.

He's a cold-hearted snake
Look into his eyes
He's been tellin' lies
He's a lover boy at play
He don't play by rules
Girl don't play the fool—no.
---Lines from the song *Cold Hearted Snake* by Paula Abdul

Chapter Three: Me, Then You

It's my life, it's now or never
I ain't gonna live forever
I just wanna live while I'm alive.
---Lines from the song *It's My Life* by Bon Jovi

Your Unalienable Right to Pursuit of Happiness

Life, Liberty and the pursuit of Happiness is a well-known phrase in the *United States Declaration of Independence*. The phrase gives three examples of the "unalienable rights" which the Declaration says has been given to all human beings by their Creator, and for which governments are created to protect. The specific phrase is "We hold these truths to be self-evident, that all men are created equal, that they are endowed by their Creator with certain unalienable Rights, that among these are Life, Liberty and the pursuit of Happiness."

Think about this for a moment. Our forefathers spent years writing this Declaration. It was agreed upon that we are all created equal, and that we all have the right to our life, our liberty, and our pursuit of happiness. No one "owns" anyone else. Your children are only under your control until adulthood. As long as you aren't breaking any laws, or any of the other Rights given by the *Bill of Rights* and/or the *U.S. Constitution*, you are free to choose your own path. You are given the freedom to choose your own route, as others are given the freedom to choose theirs.

Unless you are breaking the law, no one can take these rights away from you. You, and only you, can take away your right to pursue your own happiness. Yet some of us have become our own "jailor." We've allowed ourselves to be locked up in our own prison called self-sacrifice and co-dependency. Don't become a prisoner of war in your own mind or in your own home. Do not allow anyone to rob you of your unalienable rights!

Are You Putting Yourself Last?

The most important thing I can teach you is that you need to put yourself first. This is not being selfish – rather it is being self-full. You must be filled up with yourself in order to detach. If part of you is empty, you will try to fill that with other people. Other people will always let you down, always disappoint you, and always cause problems for you. So in order to not allow other people to bring you down, you need to be filled up with yourself so that you do not need them to fulfill you.

What does this mean, being "filled up with ourselves?" Isn't that selfish and egotistical? I was taught not to be self-centered. Family and society told me that I should be care more about others than I do about myself. I know they meant well, but they were wrong. Being "filled up with ourselves" is not about being self-centered. It is about attaching to ourselves. It is about being fulfilled within. It is about finding our true self, our core, our soul, our gifts, our desires, our needs, our passions. It is about getting to know who we are, deep down. It is about being our own best friend. It is about being happy, satisfied, and fulfilled with our "beingness." It is a spiritual pursuit, a journey into ourselves, or one could say, knowing the "God" within us.

Create Space for Your Own Best Life

The only way you can focus on yourself and your own best life is to detach from other people and their problems. You MUST let go of others in order to create space for your own life. You MUST make it a MUST. Every time you feel yourself getting sucked into other people's problems, every time you notice yourself thinking about other people's problems, you need to yell "STOP!" in your mind. I use the STOP – TRANSFER method. I say, "STOP!" then I transfer to a thought about myself. I have several thoughts I can transfer to. One of my thoughts is imagining myself at a place I'd like to go, like a health spa in Greece. One of my thoughts is how beautiful my home will look after I re-decorate and re-model it. One of my thoughts is about my goal of writing my next book.

Prepare some positive thoughts for yourself right now. Every time you get over-involved in listening to, thinking about, or feeling for others, transfer to your positive thoughts. I think Eckert Tolle has the very best formula for detachment and re-focusing back onto ourselves. When people start to talk about problems, become emotional, controlling, or guilt-inducing, or anything negative, Tolle says to not react, but to ask yourself silently, "Who am I?" Ask yourself, "What am I feeling right now?" This way you get in touch with your own feelings and you are able to protect yourself before you get sucked down someone else's rabbit hole.

Someone once said, "There are two types of business. My business and none of my business." OP's business is their business, not yours. You do not need to manage their business unless they are paying you to do so. You don't need to know about their business or even care about their business. If they choose to share it with you, great! You don't have to do anything with it or about it. Allowing them to share it with you is fine, and you can choose to listen without feeling responsible for it.

Validators vs. Invalidators

I cannot emphasize enough the power of role models, partners, mentors, sponsors, teachers and coaches. You need to surround yourself with a "team" of supporters. The word "team" represents a group of people who work together on one common goal. Your team is supporting *your* goal. Ask your teammates for support, validation and encouragement. If they aren't giving that to you, ask why.

Failure to handle this one aspect can sabotage all your best efforts! The presence of other people can either increase or decrease your desire to perform well. An example of how others can decrease motivation would be an employee who is constantly being watched and criticized by a boss while performing a task. This type of social feedback actually suppresses your ability to perform well, and will in fact cause you to err. Conversely, working on a project in a group with supportive people who all have the same goal and are depending upon each member of the group to do their part, can increase your ability to perform well.

BEWARE OF NEGATORS. The reason you don't need to put a lid on a bucket of live crabs is because they pull each other back down into the pot. There are two types of people to hang out with. Supporters or negators. Encouragers or suppressors.

Validators or invalidators. Sometimes you don't have a choice, if this person is a family member who is living with you, or if they are a boss or co-worker. When you are around an invalidator and don't have a choice, you will need to at least confront it. Being around judgmental and critical people is not only exhausting, but also anxiety provoking. Sometimes it is hard to recognize an invalidator, because a truly good one can be very covert and underhanded. Sometimes they can trick you by giving you what I call a "slap-hug." This is when they give you a compliment and a criticism at the same time. Often it is masked by humor and if confronted they will say "Oh, I was just kidding!"

The way you know if you are being invalidated is by how you feel. Have you ever felt bad around someone without knowing why? Have you ever felt confused by something someone said to you? Have you ever felt like you were walking on eggshells around a particular person? This is probably because this person has been overtly or covertly judgmental of you.

You need to get away from judgmental people as much as possible. They will suppress you and cause you a great deal of anxiety. This anxiety will block your success and forward movement. Not only that, but it if it goes too far, it will make you physically ill or cause you to get into accidents. Challenge the people in your life who are often critical. Ask them exactly what they mean. Usually there is an element of truth in criticism. Find the element of truth, agree to make necessary changes, then ask the person to let it go. Let people know that criticism is blocking your movement rather than furthering your action forward.

The people close to you are either bringing you up or bringing you down. You need to love yourself and value yourself enough that you will only allow positives into your life. We've all heard of "tough love" and how it relates to our relationships with people who are dragging us down. Yes, you need to get "tough love" with others on this issue. However, you also need to get use "tough love" with *yourself,* and follow these steps:

1. Determine who is bringing you up and who is bringing you down
2. Talk to those who often bring you down and ask for changes

3. If changes are not being made after several requests, detach from this person as much as possible

No one can make you feel inferior without your permission.
---Eleanor Roosevelt

Why Others Sabotage Us and How to Handle Them

Are you living the life YOU really want, or the life OTHERS want for you? This is a question you must ask yourself often. Your failure to handle this *one issue – sabotage by others –* can sabotage your entire achievement process!

Being too accommodating to others will impede your motivation and progress in your life. You give your power over to others when your effort toward your goals is contingent upon the participation and acceptance of other important people in your life. Moreover, it can be tempting to blame others for your own lack of movement, claiming that they will be jealous, angry, upset or overly needy if you succeed. It deprives you of your own power and autonomy. If it is others who are to blame for your failures, then these same others control your successes. This is giving away your power to others, and it is completely self-sabotaging.

One of the greatest needs of human beings is that of approval from others. Fear of disapproval is one of the greatest self-sabotages. When you are blocked because of fear of what others will think, focusing on the goal of "developing my true self" becomes a compelling replacement for the fear of "others' approval." According to Wayne Dyer, a truly self-actualized person is one who is not controlled by the opinions of others.

A well-known marketing and business consultant says, "Run, don't walk, I repeat RUN, DON'T WALK, from negative people!" But what if you *cannot* leave (or it is not in your overall best interest to leave) the people who are your greatest source of discouragement? James Prochaska discusses the idea of "enlisting" or "eliciting" helping relationships. He believes that helping relationships are of *primary value* to self-changers. He says most people in your life do *want* to help you, but do *not know how* to help you! It is up to *you* to teach your family, friends, co-workers, roommates, etc. how they can be the most helpful. It is also helpful to find a good support person or support system aside from friends and family. Examples are personal coaches, counselors, support groups, sponsors, mentors, teachers, pastors, etc.

On the other hand, you may have "supporters" who exude tremendous pressure on you to achieve a particular goal, which may or may not be *your* goal. For example, the well-meaning mother who tells her daughter, "You know you really should go into interior design. You're very artistic. You have a gift. You shouldn't let it go to waste," and so on. *Pressure creates resistance.* The more one is pressured to do something, the more difficult it seems to become. You need to set limits with people who pressure you, and again, teach them how to be supportive.

Now, here's one thing you can definitely count on. Once you've made the decision to go after your dreams, you WILL get RESISTANCE from certain people in your life! This is because you going after your dreams (or making big changes) makes certain people feel uncomfortable. Why? One reason is because it reminds them that they have given up on their own dreams. They've joined the "I've given up on my dreams club," and they want you to be in their club. You've heard that old saying, "Misery loves company." They want to be where you are, and want you to be where they are. They are afraid of separation from you.

Another reason certain people are uncomfortable with you pursuing your goals is that they are afraid of what it might do to *you*. They are afraid it might change you. They are afraid you might fail. They are afraid you might succeed. Either way, some changes are going to happen, and it will have an effect on them. They do not want their "comfort zone" disturbed. This is the way they know you, and this is what is familiar, and this is what they want to continue to count on. Most people are afraid of change.

Having some empathy for others around us who will feel the effects of our changes is important. We need to understand what they are feeling. We need to ask them what they are feeling. We need to ask for their support. It may just be the extra push that gets us through our difficult times and keeps us on our path to success.

There is something about your success that even your best friend despises.
---Mark Twain

How to Handle Criticism Without Anguish

One thing is certain. *The more successful you get, or the more you focus on your own life, the more people are going to criticize you.* You need to be prepared for this criticism. Some criticism (constructive criticism) is good for us. It needs to be heeded for us to improve and grow. But what about criticism that is unwarranted? Some people just have a critical personality. It is important to be able to distinguish between warranted and unwarranted criticism. The best way to do this is to use evaluations and statistics.

Whenever I speak I always have at least one person give me critical comments on my evaluations. I honestly ask myself if this criticism was important, warranted, genuine, and worth listening to. If I'm not sure, I will ask a trusted colleague who knows my work and I know will be honest with me. I may ask several people their opinion so I can get an idea of what a "consensus" would think. Sometimes I learn something and make appropriate changes and am grateful someone took the risk to criticize me. Other times, I determine that this person may have been competitive, jealous, angry, in a bad mood, overly irritable, or simply coming from a different reality. Either way, I don't spend much time thinking about it. I get what I need to get, then move on.

I have learned that I cannot please all the people all the time. I can please most of the people most of the time. This is my goal. Not perfection – but simply to have a positive effect on as many people as I can. I used to be very sensitive to criticism. I have learned to deal with my sensitivity by what psychologists call "individuating." This is the realization that I am a separate person. I have independent thoughts, feelings, beliefs, opinions and ideas. Sometimes I have to <u>detach, deflect, de-personalize, de-sensitize</u>. While I realize that as human beings, we are all connected and have powerful effects on each other, I have learned that sometimes I just have to be *me*.

When people show you who they are, believe them the first time.
---Maya Angelou

Choose Your People Well

The power of a support system cannot be emphasized enough. One only has to watch the "Academy Awards" and the celebrities who have climbed to the top of their profession (no easy feat!), and listen to their acceptance speeches. Rarely will they mention the difficulties, the processes, how they overcame their own sabotages and adversities – rather they spend their few moments thanking the people who supported them – and they all have them. Thanking people *in advance* for their support, validation and encouragement goes a long way in helping you achieve your goals.

When highly successful people are asked how they achieved their success they will almost always say something like, "I couldn't have done it without so-and-so." Do not underestimate the power of role models, coaches and mentors. This is why it is so important to choose your people well. The people in your life are either lifting you up or bringing you down. People can help make you or break you. You cannot afford the luxury of negative, counter, or limiting people around you. You must do everything you can to find people who are "possibility thinkers" to surround yourself with. The people around you must support you, validate you and encourage you. I recently heard Angelina Jolie on a talk show say how important it is to her to have people in her life who "elevate" her. Find people with an attitude of "abundance" rather than an attitude of "deficit."

You aren't just responsible for the energy you bring into a relationship.
You're also responsible for the energy you allow into it.
---Oprah Winfrey

Chapter Four: Your 4 Guiding Forces

In order to detach it is important to understand the mind-body-spirit connection. In every interaction and in every experience you have thoughts, feelings, and inner knowing. All your thoughts and feelings have physical consequences. Chemical messages from the brain circulate to every cell in the body, allowing your liver, heart, digestive track and immune system to eavesdrop on every mental event. Whenever you have a thought, make a decision or choice, you are affecting trillions of cells. Your physical and mental health literally depend on this mind-body-spirit connection. If you can gain power over this connection, you will let go of unnecessary anxiety, sadness, guilt and other useless emotions. You will feel fulfilled and at peace. You will feel good about yourself and the world around you. You will be physically healthier. And this is what I want for you!

We have four guiding forces inside of us that assist us in making decisions: our "head" (brains, logic, intelligence), our "gut" (intuition, soul, God within), our "chi" (life force, spirit, energy, power), and our "heart" (emotion, desire, passion). In regards to relationships, most people make mistakes when they lead with their "heart" and follow with their "gut" and their "head" and never even use their "chi." It is important to understand each of these forces and use them properly. This will assist you tremendously in detaching from anything negative or upsetting.

Lead With Your Head

When it comes to most decisions in life, we should think about it seriously and try to base our decisions on rational thought. Your "head" is your brain, or mind. If you were in an emergency situation, you would first need to be able to *think* in order to know the best way to *act*. If you don't have your "wits" about you, as in being intoxicated, over-tired, distressed, ill, or under the influence of some other substance, you will not react in the best way. In order to protect yourself and others you need to "use your head." Your "head" is your brain and your intellect. Your head needs information in order to make a good decision. Your head needs to be stable enough to weigh the pros and cons of the situation.

Your head can help protect you from getting emotionally attached to other people and their problems. Your brain can remember past events, draw information and perceive patterns. People are creatures of habit, and tend to repeat behaviors until or unless there is enough pressure or motivation for them to change. Your brain can notice these patterns and habits, and all you need to do is make a change in your thinking in order to break them. The great thing about the human brain is that it always wants to protect us. It's our emotional side that gets in the way. But the GREATER thing about the brain is that it is more powerful than our emotions, and it allows us to choose our thoughts, thereby controlling our emotions.

When you lead with your heart, you will have too much emotional vulnerability to be able to use your head and make good choices. These are times when you may need to rely on the sanity of your close friends and family. Ask the five people you trust most in your life who have your best interest in mind. Ask people who can be objective (that is, use their brains). They will be able to think of things you hadn't. They will help you see options. They can help you make changes. If you feel you don't have enough information or experience to make a good decision, ask an older person who has more information or experience to help you be rational.

Our lives are what our thoughts create.
---Wayne Dyer

Trust Your Gut

Inside each of us is an "inner knowing." It is sometimes called our "instincts," our "gut," our "soul," our "intuition," our "inner guide," or our "God within." Some call it our "sixth sense." You need to listen to this. You need to trust yourself. Trust your instincts. If you think something might not be right for you, it's not. If you sense a person is bad for you, he/she is. If you feel someone might be too controlling, he/she is. If you suspect someone is lying or cheating, he/she probably is. Your gut instinct is extremely powerful and will also work to protect you.

The only reason I didn't put "gut" before "head" is that it can sometimes be confusing. If you're not sufficiently trained and confident in knowing what your instincts feel like and what they mean, you could easily mistake them for your "heart." Sensitive people tend to lead with their hearts, and confuse their "heart" with their "soul." It's sometimes difficult to know what it is that is trying to communicate something to you. Is it my fears? Is it my general anxiety? Is it my desires? Is it my feelings? Is it my needs? Is it my selfish greed? Do I really want this or am I just being impulsive? What is really best for me in the long run? In a later chapter I will attempt to help you tune into your gut so that you can be sure what it feels like.

Anyone can cultivate their sixth sense. This is a gift to use to your advantage. Sure, you can ask all your friends what they think, and that's the best place to start when making an important decision. But we all know in our soul what is really best for us. Knowing who you are, deep down, will help you have the courage and power to stand up for yourself, detach from the world around you, and do what you need to do to take care of yourself.

How to Use Your "Chi"

What makes you happiest is living your own dream. You will never achieve your full self-actualization if you are living someone else's dream for you. You must find your own dream. Your own dream comes from your innermost core. In Eastern philosophy your core is defined as your *chi*. Chi is your life force – life energy – where your power is derived. When you are "living who you are" you will be your best self. Your chi lies below your gut. In her book *Sacred Contracts: Awakening Your Divine Potential*, Caroline Myss explains that your "sacred contract" is your higher purpose or spiritual calling. Only be connecting to our chi can we know what our higher purpose is. And we'll know we've found it because it will give us a sense of peace as well as a fire in our belly.

Your confidence and self-esteem are your greatest attributes in dealing with other people and their problems. You must find your place of "sureness," and then state it clearly and calmly. Your "chi" is your inner strength, your life force, your love energy. This is what keeps your heart beating, keeps you getting up every morning, and keeps you wanting to live. It will serve you very well. Very few people know about their chi. Most people have never even heard of it. They basically sleep-walk through life, doing what they think they should do, or what society tells them to do, or what other people want them to do. Very few people live their lives with personal intention.

When you are self-assured and self-confident, people sense your inner strength, sureness, and calm. People will normally feel safe and calm around you. We all want to know the rules, what people expect of us and how far we can push our limits. When you know yourself, others will feel they know you, and it's much easier to deal with the "known" than the "unknown." Your declarations cause people to relax. However, if you are with a controlling or manipulative person, they may try very hard to gain power over your inner power. Your inner strength may feel very threatening to this person. When they try to control or manipulate you it stems from their own fears and insecurities. If you are true to yourself, they will not be able to. You will stand tall, unwavering. You will use declarations. You will ask for what you want. You will let this person know who you are, what you want, and what you will and will not do. Your chi will kick in for you and give you this strength and power. And ironically, even the most controlling and manipulative people will back down. They will have much more respect for you and will treat you better as a result. The goal is to be as consistently "yourself" as you possibly can. Live in your deepest truth.

Your Invisible Suit of Armor

I used to have a lot of anxiety about visiting my family for the holidays. I knew someone was going to do or say something to upset me. So I started preparing in advance for how I would handle each and every situation in a calm and dignified way. It's always amazing to me that when I am prepared, armed, and ready for any possible "crap" someone could try to put on me, the "crap" never comes! It's as though I somehow show up differently, and people "sense" my strength – my readiness for battle. It's a very unconscious thing. When you are ready, others don't pull their crap. It's like you are wearing an invisible suit of armor. People only pounce when they suspect their victim is vulnerable. When you're strong, you're not vulnerable.

Our chi is our *spirit*. Our chi wants us to be alive, awake and enthusiastic. Our chi wants us to love and be loved. Our chi wants us to be healthy and live our best life. We need to be aware of our chi, bring it up to the surface, pay attention to it and nurture it. Once we do, our spirit energy will radiate to all we encounter that we are centered and on purpose.

Your dream can also be defined as your "higher purpose." To know your higher purpose, simply think about what you would like to leave as a legacy. What would you like to leave the world when you are gone? What would you most like to have others say about you when you are gone? What words do you want to have defined your life? How do you want to be remembered? Throughout this book you will be discovering more about who you are – what your passions and desires are – what puts a fire in your belly. The ultimate motivator is that fire inside of you (chi) that must be constantly kindled and flamed. YOU are way too important in this world to not find your fire and use it for your happiness and success. Then you can share it with others to improve their lives as well. Ultimately, you will be improving the world in which you live for generations to come.

To learn more about how to use your chi, check out *The Strozzi Institute* online and on YouTube. An excellent YouTube video by Richard Strozzi-Heckler on *Somatic Transformation* explains how our problems are due to being out of touch with our chi.

Nothing happens unless first a dream.
---Carl Sandburg

Follow With Your Heart

Your heart is your emotions, feelings, desires, cravings, and passions. People who are sensitive tend to get their "feelings hurt" too easily. We *react* rather than *respond*. We easily go to our place of fear. We do this when we're leading from our heart (our emotional base). Remember, we need to lead with our brain, then our gut, then our chi, then our heart. Our emotional side is important, nonetheless. If we didn't have heart, we wouldn't be able to inter-connect. We wouldn't want interpersonal relationships. We would be self-centered, solitary people. Our world would not survive if no one cared about anyone else. War is caused by people who have no heart and don't care about others.

Do not listen to people who say, "Follow your heart." When people say this (and I hear it a LOT), what they really mean is, "Do what you know is right deep down." The only way to know what is right "deep down" is to listen to your inner guide, or your soul, or your "gut." So change the saying "follow your heart" to "follow with your heart."

Some philosophers and religious teachers say we are always in only one of two states – love or fear. To me, love and fear are both in the "heart" category. And it is true that fear keeps us from being able to truly love and have compassion. Yet I feel we have many more states we can choose to be in. We can choose to be in rational thought. We can choose to be in spirit. We can choose to be in confident empowerment. We can choose the state we want to be in, and the state we choose depends on the situation and circumstances we are in, and what we are hoping to achieve.

One thing is for sure – we need to be able to love and have compassion without losing ourselves. Eastern religions teach that <u>happiness is having the ability to be compassionate as well as detached</u>. This sounds like a dichotomy, or two polar opposites, yet they can work very well together. I will explain more about how to do this later in this book.

As an example, this morning I turned on my cell phone and there was a text message from my daughter, "Everything is going wrong! My car won't start and my business phone is broken and I can't get to work or call my customers to let them know! I don't know what to do. I am just sitting here crying!" My first thought (from my anger emotion) was to write something like, "This is not what I want to wake up to on my phone! Your car and phone don't work because you thrash them, don't take care of them, and have no respect for your things! I'm not going to come over there and help you out – I'm sick of your problems! Deal with it!" My second though (from my compassion and caretaking emotion) was to write something like, "Have you called AAA? Have them tow your car to a mechanic and let me know if you need me to come get you and take you to work. Don't worry, you have insurance on your phone, we will get it fixed or get a new one."

Then I took a deep breath and asked myself, "What would a strong, confident, self-assured, empowered, loving, caring person say?" I took myself out of the "mother" role, and saw us as two equal adults. I remembered to start with my brain, then use my intuition, then my chi, and finally my heart. So I wrote, "I'm sorry to hear about all this…I'm sure you will handle it…you always do! I am sending up prayers for you now. Let me know how it goes." In this text I was able to pull myself out of the emotionality and not have her situation make me feel bad in any way. My brain and intuition told me she would be able to handle it just fine, because she has all the resources she needs, and is very strong willed and successful when she sets her mind to something she really wants. My chi gave me the strength to "Let Go and Let God." I was able to express my caring and concern without getting pulled in to any emotional drama. Surprisingly, she wrote back right away, "Thanks." I don't think this was a sarcastic "thanks," but more of a "thanks for being there and hearing me and responding to me and validating me." People just want to be heard, understood, and be validated. Sometimes they want encouragement and other types of support, but the most important thing you can do is just to listen and respond with empathy. More about empathy later!

Why You Worry and How to Stop It

According to experts in the field of anxiety disorders, mothers are the greatest worriers of all. This is partly due to the natural instinct of protection. It is partly due to a sense of overwhelming responsibility for another human life. It is partly due to the fact that most children cannot survive or function without an adult caretaker. It is partly due to society pressures, and the fact that society puts all the blame on the parents, and particularly the mother, when things go wrong with their children. *Child Protective Services* is always waiting in the wings, hovering over mothers like a helicopter looking for a criminal suspect. This, along with a multitude of other threatening people lurking around our own neighborhoods, such as kidnappers, rapists, child molesters, and drug dealers. That's not to even mention the myriad of possible illnesses, accidents and injuries that could befall our children. Many mothers think subconsciously (as I did), "As long as I'm on the job worrying, nothing will go wrong." I felt guilty when I wasn't worrying! If I was out having fun without my daughter and forgot about her for a while, then suddenly thought about her again, I would feel a horrible sense of dread. What bad thing could have happened while I wasn't worrying about her? And if something bad did happen, it's all my fault because I took my mind off her for a minute!

What happens when someone worries? Basically, they are "awfulizing" and "catastrophizing. They think of all the reasons why something might go wrong. They think of the worst case scenario. What they don't realize is that all of these negative thoughts produce negative energy, and cause it to be more likely that the awful thing will happen. If instead, they would think of all the reasons why things might go right, and anything positive that might come out of this, then "let go and let God," they would be sending out more positive energy, thus more likely to have a positive outcome.

Worry is a self-defeating behavior. It will take years off your life, will wreak havoc with your emotional health, won't protect anyone, and won't solve your problems. In fact, it interferes with your ability to make good decisions. Change the word WORRIER to WARRIOR. Change the words "I'm a worrier" to "I'm a warrior!" Change the thought "I worry too much" to "I used to worry; now I give it over to my higher power." Change the thought "I'm so worried that (whatever)," to "It's so unlikely to happen, and I have no control over it anyway, that I'm choosing to let it go."

Awfulizing and catastrophizing are the supreme self-sabotages. The great French philosopher Montaigne once wrote, "My life has been full of terrible misfortunes, most of which never happened." Anxiety distorts normal worries and magnifies them. Anxiety can be a terrible curse or an enormous blessing. It can propel us into action or it can paralyze us from movement. It can save our lives or it can cause our demise. Our expectations are extremely powerful. Work hard to change your negative expectations into positive ones! Use the following techniques to reduce your anxiety.

When you find no solution to a problem, it's probably not a problem to be solved,
But rather, a truth to be accepted.
---Anonymous

Ten Tips for Handling Anxiety

1. Keep a journal. Each day, before going to sleep, write down or say 5 to 10 things for which you are grateful for that day, and each day, after waking up, write down or say 5 – 10 things that you can give thanks for in advance.
2. Practice positive expectation by repeating positive statements to yourself.
3. Face your fears – they are not as terrible as you imagine.
4. Remind yourself of how you have already survived many challenges, and you will do it again.
5. Acknowledge your amazing potential and strive to maximize it every day.
6. Intend on being peaceful, relaxed and calm.
7. Reduce the problem to its actual size. Ask yourself "what's the worst that can happen?" Then ask "what are the chances of that happening?" If the chances are minimal, "fagetabottit!"
8. Recite the serenity prayer.
9. Let go and let God.
10. Breathe.

A ship in a safe harbor is safe, but that is not what a ship is built for.
---William Shedd

Navy Seals Stress Relief Tactics
(As printed in *O Online Magazine*, Sept. 8, 2014)

Prep for Battle:
Instead of wasting energy by catastrophizing about stressful situations, SEALs spend hours in mental dress rehearsals before springing into action, says Lu Lastra, director of mentorship for Naval Special Warfare and a former SEAL command master chief. He calls it *mental loading* and says you can practice it, too. When your boss calls you into her office, take a few minutes first to run through a handful of likely scenarios and envision yourself navigating each one in the best possible way. The extra prep can ease anxiety and give you the confidence to react calmly to whatever situation arises.

Talk Yourself Up:
Positive self-talk is quite possibly the most important skill these warriors learn during their 15-month training, says Lastra. The most successful SEALs may not have the biggest biceps or the fastest mile, but they know how to turn their negative thoughts around. Lastra recommends coming up with your own mantra to remind yourself that you've got the grit and talent to persevere during tough times.

Embrace the Suck:
"When the weather is foul and nothing is going right, that's when I think, now we're getting someplace!" says Lastra, who encourages recruits to power through the times when they're freezing, exhausted or discouraged. Why? Lastra says, "The, suckiest moments are when most people give up; the resilient ones spot a golden opportunity to surpass their competitors. It's one thing to be an excellent athlete when the conditions are perfect," he says. "But when the circumstances aren't so favorable, those who have stronger wills are more likely to rise to victory."

Take a Deep Breath:
"Meditation and deep breathing help slow the cognitive process and open us up to our more intuitive thoughts," says retired SEAL commander Mark Divine, who developed SEALFit, a demanding training program for civilians that incorporates yoga, mindfulness and breathing techniques. He says some of his fellow SEALs became so tuned-in, they were able to sense the presence of nearby roadside bombs. Who doesn't want that kind of Jedi mind power? A good place to start: Practice what the SEALs call 4 x 4 x 4 breathing. Inhale deeply for four counts, then exhale for four counts and repeat the cycle for four minutes several times a day. You're guaranteed to feel calmer on any battleground.

Learn to value yourself, which means to fight for your happiness.
---Ayn Rand

Chapter Five: Embracing Detachment

When love and skill work together, expect a masterpiece.
       ---Charles Reade

Until recently I didn't understand detachment. I only understood attachment. Why would I want to detach from people? Especially people I love and care about? It seemed like detachment meant not caring or loving others. What I've learned is that detaching is a dichotomy. When we detach emotionally, we actually are able to love more unconditionally. Other people will see that our love is not conditional on whether or not we approve or disapprove. They will feel more acceptance from us, and therefore will be able to relate to us in a healthier way.

So many of us spend so much time enmeshed in other people's problems, trying to solve or change them, that we don't really know where we end and they begin. Not reacting to people or situations that provoke us is not an easy skill to develop. It takes practice and conviction that not reacting, not increasing the drama, doesn't mean we don't care. On the contrary, we are freed to show genuine love and care only when we can detach from the knee-jerk need to fix, solve, rescue, or control. Look, taking care of one life is difficult enough! People are difficult enough without adding their personal problems! I'm here to make your life easier.

Why Detach?

Why should you detach from other people and their problems? Because it will give you *freedom* and *peace*. Here are some other great reasons:

   To love without anguish
   To have contentment
   To feel empowered
   To benefit others
   To free you from heavy emotional burdens
   To free you of responsibility
   To free you from worry

      To simplify your life
      To manage your time and energy more efficiently
      To be free from obsessive thoughts
      To feel more connected to yourself, your God, and others
      To release others to live their own lives
      To increase your faith
      To pay more attention to yourself
      To take better care of yourself
      To free up your time and energy to focus on your own best life

    Detachment is an acquired habit. It takes willingness, commitment and constant practice. Detachment is a gift you give to yourself. Attachment is imprisonment. When you are emotionally attached to others and their problems, your life begins to revolve around them. You lose yourself. They hold you hostage. Only when you detach do you keep yourself in tact.

How to Detach

    There is no one right way to detach. Since each person has a different level of sensitivity and a different level of attachment to each person in their lives, it is impossible to create a "one-size-fits-all answer. I will give you the best ways I have found.

    In order to detach you first have to get in touch with your feelings. When you feel an "irk" in the pit of your stomach, this is a sign to pay attention to. You will notice an uneasy feeling, or sensation, that something has hit a nerve. When this happens, take a moment to notice it, and see if you can label it. You might think something like, "I don't like hearing this," or "I'm feeling distressed or upset or sad or angry," or "I feel like I want to run away or lash out."

    First you have a feeling, then it translates into a thought. Once you've identified your feelings, don't automatically react. Go to your brain and ask yourself what is the best thing to do (or not do) in this situation for your highest good. You might decide that the best thing is to ignore it for now. You might decide the best thing is to confront the person about it and let them know that doesn't feel good or right to you. You might feel like you need to excuse yourself for a moment and take a bathroom break. You might feel like it's best to leave politely. If it's not the time or place to discuss it, you can always come back to this person later and bring it up. This gives you time to process it and determine what would be the best course of action.

I have found the best way for me to detach is to meditate. When I feel I need to detach from someone or something I will do a specific detachment meditation. I go to my quiet place and ask for detachment about this particular situation. I ask for guidance from God, my highest self, and my inner knowing. After 15 or 20 minutes, I always know what to do next. Sometimes it is best to do nothing. Sometimes I just give it over to God and the problem works itself through without any action on my part.

If I just need to detach from my emotions so that I can feel better, I meditate while asking God for peace. Then I erase all thought from my mind. Every time a thought comes into my mind, I breathe and transfer my attention to my breathing. If it is very difficult to get the thoughts out, I will repeat a mantra over and over in my mind. Sometimes these mantras are very helpful to think to myself when I am listening to OPP's. Here are some examples of mantras that may be helpful for you:

>NMP (Not My Problem)
>Shake it off
>I can choose peace instead of this
>I choose peace
>Let go and let God
>One day at a time
>This too shall pass
>It doesn't matter
>All is well
>Deflect, detach, de-sensitize
>Can't touch this!

Another powerful exercise is to dispute your irrational beliefs and replace them with new, positive self-statements. Martin Seligman wrote a book called *Learned Optimism*, in which he discusses the importance of cognitive restructuring. In psychology there is a concept called RBET (Rational Behavioral Emotive Therapy). The idea is to ask yourself what is the worst thing that could happen in a situation. Then ask yourself what the possibility is of that worst thing happening. It's probably not that likely, and not worthy of the amount of anxiety you place on it. Then ask yourself what is the BEST thing that could happen in this situation. Think of all the possible positive outcomes. In this exercise, you will need to use your brain. The best predictor of future behavior is past behavior. Using rational thought, experience, and statistics, you can determine the most likely outcomes. Nevertheless, at some point you may need to just take a risk and make a decision to either do nothing or confront the situation.

The 3 Main Obstacles and How to Overcome Them

There are three main things that interfere with detachment:

Obstacle #1: *I shut my body out and ignore how it feels*.
This is the most common obstacle to detachment, because there's a natural aversion to pain and discomfort. We put the small sensations that bother us out of our minds, and not until symptoms appear that cannot be ignored do we admit that there's a problem. In order to detach, you must first be willing to feel. I know that sounds like the *opposite* thing, but it is simply a *different* thing.

What you want to feel is what is going on inside of you. Get into the habit of feeling your body. Be mindful of discomfort, and pay attention to it. This is a signal that someone may be overstepping their boundaries with you. Think before you react.

Obstacle #2: *I indulge my emotions, blame them on other people and go into victim mode.*
Negative emotions are like unwelcome guests. Just because they show up on our doorsteps doesn't mean they have a right to stay. As emotions rise and fall, they merge into the river and then flow on. But if we misuse our emotions, they stick to us. Eventually, we build up a store of unhappiness, and we can become depressed.

Don't fear negativity; you can learn how to deal with it. Take responsibility for how you feel. Embrace your feelings, accept your feelings, and then let them go. Give them over to God so that you can go back to your brain and self-talk your way into feeling positive. Many of us were taught in our childhoods to be afraid of our emotions and inhibit them. Emotions were equated with losing control or embarrassing yourself. I remember stuffing back my tears all through grade school, junior high and senior high. I couldn't cry in front of my peers, lest I be made the laughing stalk of the school.

I did learn a great deal during my childhood about emotional control, however, and that was a positive thing. Emotional control doesn't mean total suppression or judging your feelings in a negative way. It means balance. Emotional balance means knowing how you feel but not being so swayed that you are ruled by every passing incident of anger, worry or resentment. The goal is, <u>to be aware of your feelings but not to be ruled by your feelings</u>. Emotions can be educated. Emotions can be trained. The only way this can happen is if you use your head, your gut, and your chi to help you.

<u>Obstacle #3</u>: *I make impulsive choices, ignore my mistakes and keep doing what didn't work in the first place, or stop doing what did work.*

All sensations, feelings, impulses and emotions must pass through our brain. When they arrive there, we make a choice. Do I follow my impulse or think about it some more? The most important part of the mind-body connection is the choice-maker, which is faced with hundreds of decisions a day, large and small. No matter what size they are, each choice gets converted into chemical messages that enter the bloodstream and inform every cell in the body. If you act impulsively on your emotions you will actually create bad habits. Habitual thinking gets imprinted into our brain like deep grooves. It becomes an addiction.

Furthermore, you must keep doing the thing that worked for you before. Tony Robbins talks a lot about success, and he has a simple success formula: *Keep doing what works and stop doing what doesn't work.* I often counsel people on how to handle a difficult person, only to hear, time after time, "I've tried everything and nothing works!" I ask them to remember a time that they dealt with this particular difficult person and handled it well, with a positive outcome. They are always able to remember at least ONE time that their communication worked. I ask them if they have tried that strategy recently, and almost always, the answer is "no." Why don't people continue doing what has worked in the past? I think it's because we are creatures of habit, and old habits die hard.

The key then, is to find out what works and keep doing it. Remember the good choices you've made. Remember a time when you were able to stop your immediate impulse to do the wrong thing, and were able to turn it around quickly. Remember your small victories. For example, when Buffy asks me for money, my natural impulse is to say something like, "I don't have any money! And you still owe me for the last thing you needed money for! I'm strapped, I'm broke, can't you see I'm struggling here???" But this is victim behavior, and I don't need to act like a victim to get what I need. So I stop and think before I respond. I have found she responds very well when I talk to her calmly and simply tell her I cannot help. I may say something like, "I wish I could, but even if I could, it would be better for you in the long run to figure this out on your own. I'm sure you will be able to, because you always do." She may not love my statement, but she does respect it, and it prevents any potential conflict.

The second key is repetition. You must repeat your positive behavior over and over. Strong willed and manipulative people will work very hard to get you off your position, and may even cause you to think what you are doing is not working. But it is very important to pause, take note of your small victory and appreciate it. In this way, you regain power and control, step by step, and become a whole person.

Most people thing the hardest three words are 'I love you,' but they're actually 'I don't know.'
---Stephen Dubner and Steven Levitt, authors of *Think Like a Freak*

Letting Go of People from our Past

As I write this book, I am hearing from various clients and friends who are having trouble letting go of people from their past. Either a deceased relative, spouse, mate, or someone they have lost who they do not see or communicate with any longer. They are asking me how to let go of the pain. They want to know how to stop dreaming about them. They don't know how to emotionally detach from the past.

I understand. I've lost my parents, many relatives, a spouse, and many boyfriends along the way. It's very difficult to lose a loved one. Sometimes we hang on to positive memories, sometimes we hang on to negative memories, and sometimes we hang on to both. We know it's over. We cannot have this person in our lives any more. Yet we still think about them, dream about them, and certain stimuli trigger memories of them. How do we let go? How do we get them out of our minds so we can focus on those who are in our lives now?

In Chapter 8 I will give you the normal stages of grieving. If you haven't gone through all of these stages successfully, the memories of this person will continue to cause you distress. Even after you've been through the grieving, you may still have distress and sadness from time to time. This is normal. You need to treat lost loved ones the same way you treat current loved ones. You need to set limits and boundaries. You need to let them know (even if in spirit) that they do not have the right to rob you of your joy and peace. You can still love them and hold them in your memory bank, but you need to rid yourself of all negative emotions related to them. Furthermore, you need to limit the amount of time you spend thinking about them. It may be helpful to say to yourself, "I'm going to allow myself to think about this person for only 15 minutes a day." It may be helpful to put all memories of them in a box or an urn and only get the box out and look at the contents during those times you have allocated to them. Some people visit gravestones, crematories or memorial places of lost loved ones periodically, which assist them in setting this limit. So you see, even people who are NOT in our lives any more physically, still need us to set limits and boundaries with them.

Think only of the positive things they did for you. Think of the positive lessons you learned from knowing them. Thank them for what you learned from them – both right and wrong. Think of them as doing the best they could with what they knew. And realize that they were put into your life for a reason. Everyone we meet is our teacher. We learn our lessons and move on. If you find you cannot move on, and are still mired down by sadness, regret or resentment, it is possible that there is a part of you that NEEDS to keep this in your life. Some people need to keep a place of sadness in their lives so they can go there and grieve. Sadness is a comforting, nurturing place sometimes. If you go there often, it becomes a familiar place, a habitual place, to grieve and mourn. It can become like a refuge, where you lick your wounds.

Just know that this is not the place God wants you to be. As long as you go to this place you will be imprisoned by your own depression. You will not be able to experience the happiness, joy, and good feelings that you deserve to feel. You can free yourself of this burden. You can "Let Go and Let God." You can ask God to help you heal. Let them go. They are gone. Live for today, live for the living, live for yourself. Focus on creating your own best life. It's okay.

Debbie Downers

You will often encounter Debbie Downers and Negative Nancy's. You don't want to spend one second longer than you have to with these people. The other night I met a man who gave me three negative statements within three minutes. He told me the people here are rude. He told me the manager here is an a-hole. He told me he had been in a horrible car accident where someone else was at fault and uninsured. He then asked me out on a date! Can you imagine? I said thank you, but I'm not available.

Another strategy that has worked well for me is something I learned from Eckert Tolle. He says when someone seems to be caught up in negativity, ask them, "What's right now?" This puts the emphasis back on the "now," which is all we have. It puts the emphasis on "right" which puts us back into a positive mindset. Recently I had a friend go on and on about all the problems in her life to the point that she started saying things like, "Why are all these bad things happening to me? Am I being punished?" I said, "What's right now?" She looked at me rather shocked and I said, "No, really. Tell me what's right in your life now." We both went on for at least ten minutes brainstorming all the things that were going well and "right" in her life right now. Her psyche went from totally negative to totally positive in ten minutes – it was amazing!

The following song lyrics are posted on the wall in my office at work. It reminds me to use my *chi*.

Roar
By Katy Perry

I used to bite my tongue and hold my breath
Scared to rock the boat and make a mess
So I sat quietly, agree politely
I guess that I forgot I had a choice
I let you push me past the breaking point

I stood for nothing, so I fell for everything

You held me down, but I got up (HEY!)
Already brushing off the dust
You hear my voice, you hear that sound
Like thunder gonna shake the ground
You held me down, but I got up (HEY!)
Get ready 'cause I've had enough
I see it all, I see it now

I got the eye of the tiger, a fighter, dancing through the fire
'Cause I am a champion and you're gonna hear me roar
Louder, louder than a lion
'Cause I am a champion and you're gonna hear me roar

Now I'm floating like a butterfly
Stinging like a bee I earned my stripes
I went from zero, to my own hero
You held me down, but I got up (HEY!)
Already brushing off the dust
You hear my voice, you hear that sound
Like thunder gonna shake the ground
You held me down, but I got up (HEY!)
Get ready 'cause I've had enough
I see it all, I see it now

I got the eye of the tiger, a fighter, dancing through the fire
'Cause I am a champion and you're gonna hear me roar
Louder, louder than a lion
'Cause I am a champion and you're gonna hear me roar
You're gonna hear me roar
Ro-oar, ro-oar, ro-oar, ro-oar, ro-oar!

Chapter Six: How to Confront Your Tightest Bonds

You Are Not Them

For the first half of my life I never knew where other people ended and I began. I didn't know what it meant to put myself first. I almost always put other people ahead of myself. I was "fused" to other people's wants and needs. I felt responsible for everyone. This became magnified times a thousand when I had my own child. We always speak in terms of "my daughter," or "my son," or "my husband," or "my sister," etc. Yet these people are not "ours." They are their own separate entities. The only thing that we own is ourselves. We can choose to be in a relationship with whomever we wish, but we can never own them.

The following is a poem that I read every single day, that has helped me more than anything to detach from my adult daughter, as well as other people in my life. It has brought me great comfort at times when I feel fearful and powerless.

Here's another important concept for you to memorize. If you don't have your own goals, other people will involve you in theirs. If you're not strong within yourself, with your own truth and self-knowing, others will weaken your resolve and pull you into their problems. Don't allow yourself to get sucked into taking care of others at the expense of yourself.

Your Children Are Not Your Children
By Khalil Gibran

And a woman who held a babe against her bosom said, "Speak to us of Children."
And he said:
Your children are not your children.
They are the sons and daughters of Life's longing for itself.
They come through you but not from you,
And though they are with you, yet they belong not to you.
You may give them your love but not your thoughts.
For they have their own thoughts.
You may house their bodies but not their souls,

For their souls dwell in the house of tomorrow, which you cannot visit, not even in your dreams.
You may strive to be like them, but seek not to make them like you.
For life goes not backward nor tarries with yesterday.
You are the bows from which your children as living arrows are sent forth.
The Archer sees the mark upon the path of the infinite, and He bends you with His might that His arrows may go swift and far.
Let your bending in the Archer's hand be for gladness;
For even as He loves the arrow that flies, so He loves also the bow that is stable.

Co-Dependency

The definition of co-dependency is enabling a person to remain a child by doing things for them that they could and should do for themselves. The reason we do this is because we have a deep-seated fear of rejection and abandonment. We think (unconsciously) that if this person needs me enough, he/she won't ever leave me. We get them dependent on us. We over-caretake and over-function. We equate love with care taking and pleasing.

The problem with this is that eventually we complain, resent and rebel. We get tired of doing "more for him than he does for me." We get tired of paying the bills, making everything work, fixing their problems. We get angry when they don't appreciate our efforts or don't take our advice or tell us to back off. Caring for others is great – but unhealthy caring shows up as controlling behavior. Besides that, when we are co-dependent it causes those around us to become selfish. Selfish people ALWAYS reject the person who tries to help them, eventually. First they reject you, then they punish you.

When we allow other people's feelings about us determine our feelings about ourselves, we will remain in distress and turmoil. When we become obsessed with "fixing" others we lose a sense of our own identity. We become emotionally enmeshed (fused) with them. Then all of a sudden, one day, we reach our limit and BANG! We want out! No warning – just GONE! It's not fair to others and it's not fair to ourselves. If there are children involved it's definitely not fair to them. So if you think you've gotten stuck in the co-dependency rut, please get help for yourself.

If you are already involved with a controlling, manipulative, alcoholic or addicted person, chances are good that you have already developed many co-dependent behaviors. Co-dependency is the need to be needed. Women often unconsciously become co-dependent in order to create a false sense of intimacy. If someone "needs" us, it must mean they "love" us. The first thing you need to "get" is that <u>need does not equal love</u>. The problem with co-dependency is that it sets up a major imbalance of power in the relationship. You give all your power away to the other person and eventually you become angry and resentful. You may complain to all your family and friends, but not be able to stop your giving. Co-dependency can become an addiction, for which you may need treatment. You are powerless over your own addiction. If you feel you are caught up in a co-dependent relationship, you need to be in recovery yourself. I recommend you attend CODA meetings. CODA stands for Codependents Anonymous, and it is based on the 12-Step Program. There are meetings every day of the week in most cities, and they are free of charge.

The concept of "powerlessness" is so significant (powerful) that it is the first step in all the 12-Step Programs. The first step then, is to accept that you are powerless over another human being. You cannot control others, you can only control yourself. Right now, you may even be powerless over controlling yourself. Co-dependency is giving yourself away (time, energy, emotion, money) to try to "help" or "fix" someone else, mainly because you need this person to stay with you or need you. Co-dependency is a toxic relationship because it erodes your self-esteem while keeping the other person in the "helpless" role. It causes you to be resentful when you "give so much" and don't get anything (or not enough) in return for all your efforts. The goal of recovery for co-dependency is to say and believe, "I cannot change another person, I can only change myself." This is the best advice anyone could ever give you.

Marriage ain't magic folks. It's managed.
---Dr. Phil

<u>Co-Dependent Meets Narcissist – The Bad Match</u>

Narcissistic personality disorder is a mental disorder in which people have an inflated sense of their own importance and a deep need for admiration. Those with narcissistic personality disorder believe that they're superior to others and have little regard for other people's feelings. But behind this mask of ultra-confidence lies a fragile self-esteem, vulnerable to the slightest criticism.

Being self-centered is a more mild form of narcissism. Self-centered people think the world revolves around them and they have a heightened sense of self importance. The main difference is that self-centered people can learn to have empathy and care about other people, and can be taught how to share and give.

It is important to know that for the purposes of this book I use the term *narcissist* loosely. Usually when I refer to a narcissist, I'm referring to narcissistic *behaviors*. There is a difference between "behaving narcissistic" and actually having narcissistic personality disorder. Narcissistic personality disorder is one of several types of personality disorders. You need to know that personality disorders are very difficult to treat because usually the person doesn't believe he/she has a problem.

Self-centered and narcissistic people always seem to match up with dependent and co-dependent people. You will be the pole that they magnetize to. You need to identify if this person is self-centered or narcissistic. If they are self-centered, it very well could be that you've helped form that by giving too freely. You will need to use the strategies I outline for you below, particularly setting limits and boundaries. If the person responds to these strategies, there is hope. If the person refuses to accept your limits and boundaries, and fights you with hostility, it could be that they have a personality disorder over which you have no control.

Personality disorders are conditions in which people have traits that cause them to feel and behave in socially distressing ways, limiting their ability to function in relationships and in other areas of their life, such as work or school. Narcissistic personality disorder is diagnosed based on signs and symptoms, as well as a thorough psychological evaluation that may include filling out questionnaires. Some features of narcissistic personality disorder are similar to those of other personality disorders. It's possible to be diagnosed with more than one personality disorder at the same time.

This book is not about diagnosing or treating problematic behavior. It is about empowering you to handle difficult people. Narcissistic personality disorder can only be diagnosed by a trained therapist or physician. Below are some of the signs and symptoms of a narcissistic and/or self-centered personality.

Believing that you're better than others
Believing that you're intellectually superior
Fantasizing about power, success and attractiveness
Exaggerating your achievements or talents
Expecting constant praise and admiration
Failing to recognize other people's emotions and feelings
Expecting others to go along with your ideas and plans
Taking advantage of others
Expressing disdain for those you feel are inferior
Being envious or jealous of others
Believing that others are jealous of you
Trouble keeping healthy relationships
Setting unrealistic goals
Being easily hurt and rejected
Having a fragile self-esteem
Appearing as tough-minded or unemotional
Having an exaggerated sense of self-importance
Being preoccupied with fantasies about success, power or beauty
Believing that you are special and can associate only with equally special people
Requiring constant admiration
Having a sense of entitlement
Behaving in an arrogant or haughty manner

    Narcissism crosses the border of healthy confidence and self-esteem into thinking so highly of yourself that you put yourself on a pedestal. In contrast, people who have healthy confidence and self-esteem don't value themselves more than they value others.
    If you feel you are with someone who doesn't value you, your needs, requests, time, money or energy, you are probably with a self-centered or narcissistic person. You may feel belittled by this person, or looked down upon as inferior. The person may have a sense of entitlement. When they don't receive the special treatment to which they feel entitled, they may become very impatient or angry.
    Another thing to watch out for is inconsideration. The definition of "inconsiderate" is one who does not consider your

needs, desires or feelings when acting and making decisions. If you've told this person several times you do not like or want a certain behavior, and they keep doing it, clearly this person is devaluing you. At this point you need to be very strong and let the person know that if they cannot respect your wishes, you cannot be around them.

There are three classes of men; lovers of wisdom, lovers of honor, and lovers of gain.
---Plato

Co-Dependency vs Empathy

Empathy is the ability to listen to another person with caring and concern, letting them know you understand what they are telling you, and showing compassion for them. One way to show empathy is to respond with something like, "I hear you." Sometimes this is the only thing the person wants from you. Empathy is non-judgmental. Empathy does not try to advise, fix, help, control, or convince. Empathy is not sympathy, and does not get sucked into other people's issues with emotion. Empathy does not respond with emotion. Empathy responds with eye contact, complete attention, and in a way that the person feels heard. Empathy simply listens in an understanding way. People pay hundreds of thousands of dollars to therapists, just to have someone listen to them with empathy.

Empathy is a skill that takes practice. The main difference between co-dependency and empathy is that you have no emotional investment in the other person's issue. You do not try to "help." If the person asks for your advice, first ask what ideas they have considered. If they still need advice, you could offer some ideas. Empower the person by letting them know that they have all their own answers deep inside them. Ask them to pray or meditate and see what comes up. Let them know it's okay to get back to you if they still feel they need some direction. If you have listened to the same story over and over, and it appears this person is stuck or resistant to taking positive action, you may need to direct them to someone who is in the "helping role," such as a counselor, coach, clergy, supervisor, mentor, teacher, etc.

I'm assuming here that this person is not so disturbed that you feel threatened by them. If you feel this person might retaliate or become revengeful, or try to hurt you in some way, you need to contact someone who can help YOU. You may need to call the police, call a counseling hotline, get a restraining order, or take extra security measures. If you feel you may be in a threatening situation, read my book, *The Romantic Terrorist: How to Protect Yourself from Stalkers, Bullies, and Other Threats.*

I'm not striving to perform perfectly; I'm just looking for harmony.
--Ellen Gibson

The Cure: Respect, Reality and Reciprocity

Respect

You must expect <u>respect</u>. Boundaries are your primary form of protection. Do not be afraid of the consequences when you set limits. Don't be afraid to call people out on their disrespect. Depending on the severity of the disrespect, most people will actually respect you much more and treat you much better when you let them know the rules. Saying something like, "It's very important to me that (whatever)" is a great way to start your conversation. If he/she says you're making too big a deal about something, or you're being over-sensitive, just say, "If it's important to me it should be important to you."

The way to be less vulnerable (and sensitive) with others is to be more self-protective. The "180 degree turn" is one of the best strategies in difficult negotiations. A wise person once told me, "Be committed but not attached." When you say what you want, be willing to let go of the outcome. If the person insists it has to be his/her way, just say "Okay, I guess we'll have to forego this activity." Leave it at that and LEAVE. Likely he/she will come around to your side eventually – that is, if he/she wants to be with you bad enough. In fact, the closer bond you have with this person (as in spouse or family member) the more likely they are to come around.

Be strong enough to say "no" and mean it. I once saw a headline on the cover of Time Magazine that read "How to Say 'No' to Your Kids." I bought it, because I really wanted to know how to do it! A male friend of mine saw the magazine on my table and said, "I'll tell you how to say 'no' to your kids – put a 'hell' in front of it!" I laughed, but it made sense. The main thing is that you should only have to say "no" once. If the person doesn't respond, you need to set a limit or a boundary. For example, if you ask your teenager to put his/her clothes away and he/she says, "no," you could say, "I expect these clothes to be put away within five minutes or I will need to dump them in the trash." Then you have to be strong enough to follow through on your word. Do this same thing at least three times, and you won't have trouble with it any more.

Reality

One of the most common therapeutic techniques therapists use with clients who are "living in a fantasy world" is *reality testing*. Reality testing is simply pointing out the reality of the situation and asking the person if they understand that. If they refuse to accept reality, it is explained that they are going to have a difficult time in life when they hold on to falsehoods, hopes, dreams, and "maybe someday's."

Sometimes we can let it go and allow them to have their dreams. Other times it is important that we point out the facts. It really depends on whether or not their un-reality has a direct effect on you. It is important for others around you to see you as someone who is real, and in touch with reality. You need to show up as stable, secure, confident, calm and strong. When you show up this way, most people will not question you.

If there is a debate and you know that you are right about something and the other person is wrong, best way is simply to present the waterproof evidence to them and then walk away, without too much explanation. If you start to talk about things or debate with them, they can magically turn things around and make it sound as if you misunderstood them, that they actually meant the same as you, but you just misinterpreted it. If the person gets angry or hostile, the best thing to do is simply leave them alone until they've calmed down. Do not be afraid to leave or ask them to leave. If you ask someone to leave your home, they need to respect your wishes and leave immediately. If they do not, then you need to leave. Then call the police for assistance.

Reciprocity

Reciprocity is about give and take. In conversations, it is a two-way street. If you notice someone is dominating conversations and activities you will need to talk with him/her about it. You might say something like, "I've noticed that when we're in a group setting you tend to dominate the conversation and I would like you to give other people a chance to talk more." If he/she asks what you mean, you could say, "Sometimes you interrupt people, including me, and it feels like disregard. Sometimes when others are telling a story, rather than commenting about their story, you start telling a similar story of your own and it changes the whole dynamics of the conversation. It causes me and maybe other people to feel that what we have to say isn't important to you. Do you understand?" If he/she gets defensive, just say, "Ok, I can see that either you don't get what I'm saying, or you don't like that I'm saying it. I would just like you to take it into consideration." See what he/she does the next time you're socializing. If he/she doesn't change, he/she really has disregarded you.

<u>Whatever behavior you're willing to tolerate is exactly what you'll get</u>. So if you don't like being dominated, you need to ask for reciprocity. It's not fair to complain to everyone you know about someone's behavior but not tell that person directly that it bothers you and not give that person a chance to fix it. If you've told him/her about the problem and he/she doesn't fix it, there's a bigger problem. Let the person know the behavior you expect and if they don't comply, either ask them to meet you in counseling, ask for a break, or simply choose to not be around this person any more (or as little as possible).

When someone is not reciprocal in a relationship you need to confront it. Again, it could very well be that this person has become accustomed to you doing all the work. If you've asked for compromise and more give-and-take, and the person staunchly refuses, it can be very distressing and confusing. You don't understand why the person refuses to do anything to save your relationship when he/she claims to love you so much. He/she rejects you and at the same time asks you to be supportive and understanding of him/her. You may wonder if you did something wrong. You may try to recapture the bond you once had that has begun to erode. You may feel you're going insane. You may be like a "love-sick crack addict."

Once you see this inconsistency, you need to confront it. <u>You need to say who you are, what you want, and what you'll do if you don't get it</u>. You must be very matter of fact and very specific with a self-centered person. If you are wishy-washy at all they will sense your weakness and pounce on it or use it against you. After you've been clear about what you want and expect, ask for their commitment to it. If the person does give you a commitment to change and it continues, you need to leave. The 180 degree turn is the most effective negotiation strategy. You don't necessarily have to leave forever. Sometimes just a few minutes is effective, sometimes a few days, sometimes a few weeks, sometimes longer.

Enabling

Enabling is another fancy word for co-dependency. There is a big difference between "helping" and "enabling." Enabling is not helping! Enabling makes the situation worse, not better. Enabling has to do with the following:

Doing things for others that they can (and should) do for themselves, i.e., cleaning up their messes, paying for their messes, bailing them out of their messes, lying or "covering up" for them
Making excuses for and/or defending bad behavior
Coddling and babying when bad behavior is accompanied by sorrow and playing "victim"
Allowing them to live with you without financial responsibility
Allowing them to maintain their addiction and continue a relationship with you by not requiring them to get into treatment
Accepting their apologies and promises to change over and over
Allowing them to take advantage of you
Allowing them to treat you with disrespect
Allowing them to "use" you, your home, car, environment, etc.
Calling every therapist, counselor, or treatment program in town to try to find one best for them

Actual Helping Behaviors

Showing empathy and concern for their well being

Asking if they would like your assistance in making a good decision for themselves
Attending Al-Anon or CODA meetings on your own
Setting firm limits with them about what you will or won't tolerate and meaning it
Taking care of yourself and focusing on yourself
Leaving the situation when you are being disrespected

Boundaries That Promote Intimacy

When setting limits with a loved one, it is important to attempt to keep your bond in tact. When you confront your loved one, think about it first and be sure it's something important. Express your issue in a timely fashion – as soon as possible after the infraction – at a time when you'll be sure you'll have your loved one's undivided attention and they are in a good space. First express appreciation for your loved one's intent to please you. Assume this person loves you and wants you to be happy. Ask your loved one to respect your feelings and requests. Speak as honestly as possible, and come from a place of love rather than anger. Here are some other ideas that may be helpful.

Ask the person to listen to you without distraction or interruption
Respect the person's requests for space
Allow each other to be individuals
Make important decisions that affect both of you, together
Negotiate conflicts in as fair a manner as possible – ask the person to give up something if you are asked to give up something
Make amends when the person has suffered as a result of something you've done, even if you think he/she "shouldn't" feel this way
Remember that "feelings" are not right or wrong – they just are – do not judge others' feelings
When something is important to you it should also be important to your loved one – ask them not to minimize, demean or deny your feelings
When your loved one does something you like, let him/her know you appreciate it

Stay calm and mature in your discussions – avoid anger, defensiveness, hostility and rage

Don't criticize the other person, just say what has upset you and ask for positive change

Respect each other's privacy – don't read each other's phone texts, emails, mail or anything else – even if it's left lying around open

Use "I statements," i.e., "When you are late without calling to let me know it makes me feel like I'm not important to you and my time is not important to you."

After you've stated your concern, offer a solution, i.e. "In the future I'd like you to call me as soon as you know you may be late," or ask the person for a solution, i.e. "What do you think we can do about that?"

Allow the other person to come up with ideas for solving problems – often they will come up with much better ideas than you had. When your loved one says he/she has a "better" way of doing things, listen and determine if that would work for you before you agree to it. If you don't want to do it that way, say so. By the same token when you feel you have a "better" way of doing things than your loved one, be careful of suggesting it – it may be received as criticism and rejected. If you do suggest it, let go of their decision about whether or not to do it "your way" (unless it directly affects you).

If you sense your loved one is responding negatively or in a hostile way when you are trying to have a mature discussion, confront him/her on it immediately, then leave if necessary to avoid further escalation. If you aren't sure what to do or say, ask for some time – let your loved one know you will think about it and get back to him/her within an appropriate period of time. If your loved one isn't ready to talk or negotiate, ask if you can schedule a time that would be better for him/her.

I love the term "strong surrender." All you have to do is three simple things: state the problem, state what you want, and ask for his/her suggestions. Then, physically lean back. Let him/her respond. Listen and nod in understanding. Then restate what you want. Be a broken record if you need to be. Don't allow him/her to pull you into a verbal conflict or change the subject. Your goal is to state your peace, then solve the problem. If he/she still refuses to surrender (surrendering means accepting the problem and working through it to resolution in a calm, rational manner), offer to leave until he/she is ready. Remember, your absence will have more power than your presence in resolving this problem!

Stop the Insanity!

The biggest problem people have with the people they love is <u>obsessive rumination</u>. They obsess over the other person's problems. They obsess over their relationship, their conversations, wondering if they said the right thing, wondering if they should tell them more, wondering what happened and how they might have prevented it, and on and on. They obsessively ask "Why?" They obsessively talk to their friends about it while trying to figure out why they did what they did, why they said what they said, why they are the way they are, why they didn't love us the way we loved them, why, why, why? They need to *know*.

Well, I'm here to tell you, you DON'T need to KNOW. It doesn't matter why. He/she is who he/she is. They did what they did. You did what you did. Ruminating won't change anything – it will only keep you wallowing in pain and misery. Yes, you need to use your brain, but not to obsess over the "why?" Some people think that if they can just understand why a person is the way he/she is, or why a person does what he/she does, this will magically make everything better. I'm here to tell you that it WON'T make it better. You don't have to explain it to yourself, to them, or to anyone else. The quicker you get to acceptance of "what is," the quicker you will be able to detach and focus back onto yourself.

When I was raising my daughter I would talk to friends and family about our struggles. They would inevitably ask "Why does she do that?" Trying to explain why someone does what they do is like trying to nail jello to the wall. Particularly in the case of teenagers! What I finally learned to say is, "I don't know and I don't care. It doesn't matter. Knowing what causes it won't make it better. I just need someone to listen and assist me in finding ways to manage it." Don't get sucked into other people asking you *why* someone is acting a certain way. Often this will lead you down the quicksand of "It must be my fault." How people choose to behave is never your fault. You may have acted in a way that encouraged negative behavior, but it is still not your fault. Get rid of the guilt and move on toward problem solving!

When you find yourself ruminating, immediately yell, "STOP" in your mind, and transfer to a positive thought. Say to yourself over and over, "It doesn't matter, it doesn't matter, it doesn't matter." Stop the insanity!

Buffy is a prime example of constant drama and emotional upheaval. I've learned to de-sensitize to her "stuff," as she over-emotes about everything. Well, not everything. She makes a huge dramatic deal about losing her cell phone charger but no expression whatsoever when she hears about a mass shooting spree on the news. I've learned this is common with teenagers and young adults, particularly with females. They are in their own little worlds and only seem to care about themselves and their connection to their friends, boyfriends, cars and social activities. I get that. The problem is that I have to brace myself every time I see a phone text or call from her. I take a deep breath, and say to myself, "All is well." About half of her contacts are something about a problem in her life. I know I don't have to fix her problems, and I've learned to say things like, "You can do this," and "You can figure this out," and "This too, shall pass." I no longer soak up her emotions like a sponge. I wear my bullet-proof vest and let the problems and emotions bounce off me.

Last night Buffy asked me for money. This was the 4th time in one month. I had said "no" to the first three requests, but she wore me down on the fourth one, which was losing her cell phone (again). I went against my "battle plan" and gave my credit card number to the insurance agent over the phone. I felt overwhelmed, angry, depleted, and frustrated once again.

I tell myself I'm improving, because I was able to say "no" three times out of four, and it was only $50 which I tell myself isn't the National Debt. I make all kinds of justifications in my mind, like she needs her phone to work, she needs to work to make money, she needs a phone in case of emergency, she needs a phone in case my granddaughter has an emergency, etc., etc., etc. But the reality is, here I go rescuing her again. Super-Mom to the rescue again. I'm wondering if a "good" mom helps her adult kids out of trouble or if a "good" mom makes her adult kids figure out how to keep themselves out of trouble.

I've got to stop the insanity. I accept that I'm not perfect, and I'm learning to become stronger every day. I do the best I can with what I know, and leave the outcome in God's hands. I cannot play God. God has a plan for my life and a plan for every other person's life. The only way to stop the insanity is to "Let Go, and Let God." Then I recite the serenity prayer which is attributed to the 12-Step Programs:

God, grant me the serenity to accept the things I cannot change, the courage to change the things I can, and the wisdom to know the difference.

Get Fed Up!

When I did research for this book, I asked all my friends and relatives "How do you detach from other people and their problems?" I got a variety of answers, but one that kept coming up was "anger." People said that things won't change until they get mad enough, frustrated enough, or "fed up." For some this means "hitting bottom." Anger is a strong emotion. Anger can create passion. One must be careful about anger, however. While anger is a normal, useful emotion, it can be self-destructive if allowed to go too far or out of control.

The most important thing about anger is to recognize it early on. You need to get out of denial about your anger, and ask yourself what you are angry about. If you deny your anger it will get pent up. Pent up anger is like a pressure cooker. It gets stronger and stronger until one (often tiny) thing will set it off and it will blow. Blowing up is always self-destructive and/or other-destructive.

On the other hand, many people never blow up, they just hold anger in and turn it against themselves. Depression is anger turned inward. Depression causes fatigue and loss of motivation. Therefore, it is extremely important that you become aware of your anger and frustration before it turns against you. Depression is the psyche's weapon of mass destruction (WMD).

Anger can be used as a powerful change agent if used in a positive way. Anger is important because it warns us and protects us from hurt and pain. Here's how to use anger as a positive force. First, you need to take some time each day to meditate or relax and ask yourself if you are angry about anything in your life. If so, you need to put it into words to yourself, for example, "I'm angry when my teenager asks me for rides at the last minute." Second, you need to determine how you can and will set limits with yourself or others in order to handle your anger effectively. Third, you need to state your new limit (or commitment) to yourself and to others if they are involved. For example, you might say to yourself "I will no longer give rides to my teenager unless I get at least 10 hours advanced notice and it is convenient for me." Then you might say to your teenager, "I will no longer give you a ride unless I get at least 10 hours advanced notice, and then only if it is convenient for me."

When you notice you are uneasy after a communication with anyone, pay attention to the uneasiness. See if you can define it. Are you shocked, annoyed, irritated, hurt, angry? Recently after an hour long phone call with a friend I realized I was really angry. This was the third time this week she had spent an hour of my time venting and spewing all her emotional drama, while I barely said three words. I felt like someone had just barged into my home and threw black paint all over it. And then I thought, what would I do if someone really did throw black paint all over my home? I would, of course attempt to get them to leave. I would yell at them to "STOP!" I would call the police if I had to. So what's the difference? When someone is spewing their troubles all over you, time after time, should you just sit there and accept it? Absolutely NOT. You should get MAD!

There is a famous line in a movie where a man yells out the window of his apartment, "I'm mad as hell and I'm not going to take it anymore!" This can be a life-changing statement. Simply stating aloud that you are FED UP and have reached your limit is very powerful. If anger motivates you, use it in a positive way and it will be your friend.

If there is no struggle, there is no progress.
---Frederick Douglass

Chapter Seven: What to Do When You've Reached Your Breaking Point

My method is to take the utmost trouble to find the right thing to say, and then to say it with the utmost levity.
--George Bernard Shaw

How to Not Crack Under Stress

What does it mean when you find yourself saying or thinking "I can't take this anymore." We've all been there, yet these words don't mean the same thing to everyone. People reach their breaking point in different ways, according to their personalities. A person who balks under pressure may just stop responding entirely. Another person simmers, and then suddenly explodes. Everything depends on how you relate to stress, because reaching the breaking point happens when your ability to cope with stress breaks down.

There are two main types of stress: *acute stress* and *chronic stress*. *Acute stress* is something immediate, which happens all at once, when you're in an auto accident, or are frightened by something, or hear bad news. These events trigger the stress response very quickly, releasing hormones associated with the fight-or-flight response. You will be tempted to fight or run (or get help). *Chronic stress* builds up over time. It is more like hearing a dripping faucet. First you notice it, then you get irritated and finally you can't stand it anymore. You crack. And "cracking" is different for everyone.

There are normally three stages of stress. In the first stage, you are aware of being under pressure, either time pressure, self-pressure or pressure from others. There is a mild feeling of anxiety, or a pit in your stomach. Yet you still feel you can handle it. In the second state, you're feeling frazzled. You're off center. You forget things, feel dizzy, can't pay attention. You have to make a conscious effort not to respond with anger and impatience. In stage three, you can't cope any longer. Something triggers you and you have an outburst, which releases your tension momentarily, but leaves you with feelings of embarrassment, guilt and regret.

For some chronic stresses, reducing or eliminating the root cause is the solution. Not taking action is like walking around for days with a rock in your shoe thinking, "I can stand this. I just have to work through the pain," when what is called for is taking the rock out. If something in your life—your work, a relationship, a financial strain—is causing you to reach the breaking point more than once or twice, you need to look seriously at making a significant change. Putting up with chronic stress is bad for both mind and body. The brain's stress response isn't set up to be triggered constantly, and the presence of stress hormones like adrenaline and cortisol over an extended period throws your whole physiology out of balance.

The most effective strategy for diminishing chronic stress is to begin at stage one, and not let it get to stage two or three. In order to do this, you have to listen to your gut. When you get irritated, annoyed, or a feeling of angst, you will know this is your warning sign. <u>Something's got to give</u>. You need to get centered and back in balance as quickly as you can. How do you do this? It all happens in consciousness. You need to learn what it feels like to be centered. You need to value this state. You need to train your brain to stay there.

Being centered has a set of feelings associated with it. Physically, you are calm but not dull or fatigued. Inside your calmness you feel alert and alive, with more than enough energy to do what you need to do. You've had a good night's sleep. Your mood is up. If you place your attention in the center of your chest, in the region of the heart, there's a sense of openness. Nothing hurts anywhere in your body. This is a state of being present, or "being in the now."

You can achieve this state through relaxation. You will need to force yourself to sit or lay down, let every muscle in your body relax, take some slow deep breaths, and get in touch with your inner guide. I will explain more about this in a later chapter.

In the meantime, take care of yourself. Here are some of the ways I've found are best for me to take care of myself:

Get counseling or coaching
Get into a support group
Talk to supportive friends and family
Go to church
Pray

Meditate
Get massages, facials, manicures and pedicures
Go to a spa
Join a gym and go daily
Spend an hour in a hot tub
Take a hot shower or bath
Attend CODA or Al-Anon meetings at least twice a week
Read good books
Write in your daily journal
Go see movies (not sad or romance movies!)
Take dancing lessons
Take up a new sport or hobby
Decorate your house
Throw a dinner party
Visit your long lost relatives
Plan a vacation
Take a weekend trip – even if it's alone
Take a course or class in something you're interested in
Start a walking group

Tough Love

The only way to get off the "yo-yo" merry-go-round with OPP's is to grow some <u>ovaries or testicles of steel</u> and get <u>tough love</u> with yourself. You must believe you deserve more than this. You must believe you deserve better than this. You must create space for your own best life. You MUST make it a MUST. You must get tough love with yourself before you can get tough love with others. Once you've set appropriate limits and boundaries with others, you need to stick with them, no matter how uncomfortable it gets. I think the older we get, the more we are able to "tough love." Here is a quote I love from Meryl Streep, on getting older and wiser.

I no longer have patience for certain things, not because I've become arrogant, but simply because I reached a point in my life where I do not want to waste more time with what displeases me or hurts me. I have no patience for cynicism, excessive criticism and demands of any nature. I lost the will to please those who do not like me, to love those who do not love me and to smile at those who do not want to smile at me. I no longer spend a single minute on those

who lie or want to manipulate. I decided not to coexist anymore with pretense, hypocrisy, dishonesty and cheap praise. I do not tolerate selective erudition nor academic arrogance. I do not adjust either to popular gossiping. I hate conflict and comparisons. I believe in a world of opposites and that's why I avoid people with rigid and inflexible personalities. In friendship I dislike the lack of loyalty and betrayal. I do not get along with those who do not know how to give a compliment or a word of encouragement. Exaggerations bore me and I have difficulty accepting those who do not like animals. And on top of everything I have no patience for anyone who does not deserve my patience.
---Meryl Streep

Create a Strategy

This past New Year's Day I made a "New Year's Resolution." I would carve out time to do at least three things a day that are good for me without letting anyone stop me. I realized I had been neglecting my health, my diet, my exercise, my church, my home repairs, my car repairs, my teeth, my skin, my hair, my nails, etc. I had even stopped taking my vitamins and making my morning fruit smoothies because it was taking too much time! Seriously??? I had to really look at what my priorities were. I say my physical, mental and spiritual health and safety are my first priority, but I certainly wasn't acting that way! So I started making appointments to fix all of these things. I can't tell you how much this has changed my life! Scheduling "good for me" time has helped me more than anything to set appropriate limits and boundaries with others. It's made me feel good about myself – even proud of myself. Each thing I do for myself that promotes my health and safety I give myself a "high-five" for.

What I have learned is that I have to <u>first</u> look at myself. I first need to take good care of myself and manage my own life well. I need my own life to be <u>cleaned up</u>. Then I will show up as someone who cares, who pays attention, who values herself and her life, and who others will see as a role model. When me, my home, my car, my finances, my activities are all well-managed, others notice it. The message is something like, "I don't live a messy life, so if you're a mess, go somewhere else."

<u>Second</u>, I need to stand confident and be willing to speak up and say what I want. Rather than wait for someone else to mess up, I need to state how I want it to go. I now make declarations such as, "It's going to be a great day!" or "When we get home we will take our showers, have dinner, and be in bed by 9pm." I need to clean up the messes I have with other people. I need to make sure I'm getting treated with respect by every single person I have contact with.

<u>Third</u>, I need to pay attention to what is happening around me. This is not to say that I need to be like a police officer looking for trouble, but I need to be aware of what's going on, how others around me are behaving, and stay conscious to the moment.

<u>Fourth</u>, I need to confront potential problems right away. I need to have the courage to ask people for change, to show disapproval, and to state how I want my life to be. I have to remind myself that I am a human being with the right to live her life the way she wants. If that means others around me need to modify their behavior, so be it.

Choose Every Battle

Arm yourself for battle with your "higher self." When you come from a place of "no tolerance" people will feel it. It is an invisible bullet proof vest. It comes from your chi energy. It can't be seen, but people will pick up the "vibes" you give off. I used to give off the vibe, "Take advantage of me." Now I give off the vibe, "You can't touch this!"

I've learned to choose every battle. This doesn't mean that every little problem needs to become a battle. What it means is that I need to pay attention to every little thing that is a problem for me. Sometimes it's best to let it go. But most of the time it's best to confront the little things so they don't become big things. When I am "picky" about the little things, people get a "knowing" that I will definitely NOT TOLERATE the bigger things. If they don't like that I'm "on top of it" they will gravitate elsewhere. But it's interesting, I've noticed that the more I've gotten on top of myself and others, the more they want to be around me. I've noticed people congratulating me on my new strength and courage. So far, my new attitude has created a far more positive, peaceful life!

Have High Standards

High standards are your protective gear. You need to be a person with high standards and class. You need self-respect. You need to be respected by all people in your life, and the only way to be respected is to have standards. Children don't respect their parents when they don't have high standards (or don't implement them). Employees don't respect their employers when they don't have high standards. People don't respect people who don't have high standards.

So <u>raise your standards</u>, NOW. Stop tolerating abuse and disrespect from all people in your life. <u>Lower your tolerations</u>. <u>Raise your demands</u>. It's not about being a bitch, it's about knowing who you are and standing up for that. Never feel bad about saying who you are and what you want. Never, ever allow anyone to make you feel stupid, childish or inferior for saying who you are and what you want. Let's start right now. State this to yourself. "I am a person of integrity with high standards and class. I calmly and clearly state who I am and what I want. I expect to be respected for that."

If they hadn't tried to break me down, I wouldn't know that I was unbreakable.
---Gabourney Sidibe

When to Amputate

Only you know when it is time to break off a relationship. Obviously, you need to consider the consequences. Much depends on the nature of the relationship. The most difficult relationships to break off are with our children or our parents, because these are the relationships we are most deeply emotionally bonded with. When it comes to family, I suggest doing everything in your power to salvage some type of relationship, even if it is simply being cordial around each other. If possible, try to get some professional help before deciding to break off a relationship with a spouse, mate or family member.

Friends and associates are another whole issue. Generally I gauge the relationship on how much I feel bad versus how much I feel good. Remember, people are either bringing you up or bringing you down. So you need to look at the percentage of time you feel good, elevated, uplifted, empowered, validated, supported and encouraged by this person. Then look at the percentage of time you feel degraded, criticized, disrespected, demeaned, devalued, or distressed.

Steve Harvey says, "When I hear another person's problems I offer them a few ideas as to how they could solve them. If they find something wrong with it; find every reason why it won't work, I immediately end the conversation. The moment I hear, 'I don't think that will work," I say, 'Okay, thank you,' and I'm gone." As the saying goes, "Misery loves company." You don't need to be their company. You can choose to let go and detach. You must protect yourself from getting pulled down into the misery cycle. You have to know when to let go of someone who insists on being miserable and staying miserable. You need to be happy and feel good!

I have had to let go of many friends throughout my life. One example is a friend who I felt was extremely demanding and self-centered. When we would get together, it always had to be at a place she wanted to go and at a time that was convenient for her. She was chronically late – up to an hour sometimes. She wouldn't call to let me know she was going to be late until she knew I was already at our meeting place. She often cancelled at the last minute. She insisted we share a meal, and she insisted on ordering what she liked, without regard for my preferences or budget. When I would tell her I wanted something different, she insisted we share both items. The entire time we were together she monopolized my time and the conversation, even when we were at a party where there were other people. She had a host of problems which she wanted me to solve for her. When I told her I couldn't tell her what to do she got angry. When I gave her a suggestion she would insist she couldn't do that. When I finally confronted her about these things, she became defensive and told me I was over-reacting. I simply said I felt we were too different and that our get-togethers felt more like work to me than fun. She kept calling me leaving messages on my voice mail. I ignored them and she eventually went away. Sometimes I still run into her when I'm out, and I am polite, but don't spend any more time with her than I need to.

There will be times when you need to confront a person and be honest and up front about why you want to end the relationship or take a break. If you feel this person would not respond well to your truth, and would further disrespect you or try to make you feel bad, it might be best to just ease out of the relationship slowly. You could simply become too busy. If the person asks why you have backed off you should be honest but keep it short and sweet. You could say something like, "I only have so much time, energy and resources, and I have too many other people in my life who take that out of me. I simply don't have enough to go around." You are not making them "wrong" or "bad," you are just letting them know you have other priorities. Which is the truth.

When you break up with a person you've known or been with for a long time, it can feel like an amputation. Sometimes, the only way to stop the "bleeding" is to "amputate." When doctors are making a decision as to whether or not to amputate a person's limb, they base their decision making on the best interest of the patient's <u>overall health and wellbeing</u>. This is what you should do also. You need to look at the <u>big picture of your life</u>. Is keeping this person in your life causing you distress, upset, or illness? Is having this person in your life keeping you from being as healthy and successful as you could be? Would keeping this person cause you to be unhealthy in any way? Would the loss of this person cause you to be more or less healthy?

Amputating means cutting him/her out of your life. Your inner self knows whether or not you should do this. Of course, whenever there is an amputation, it takes time for the injury to heal. The body may go through many painful reactions while it is recovering and re-balancing. The patient may go through a period of emotional distress, depression, and despair. They will go through a grieving process just as though they had lost a significant other. It will take time, good medical care, and plenty of social support for the person to fully recover, accept and integrate into their new life. So yes, for a while, you may be in more pain than ever before. Yet for the <u>long run</u>, you may have just saved your life.

When you break up with someone, make it sure and swift.
---Dr. Drew

Normal Stages of Grieving

The pain associated with ending of a relationship is a long, slow experience – a set of grieving stages that one goes in and out of, not necessarily in this order:

Denial
Anger
Bargaining
Disappointment, sadness and depression
Acceptance
Healing
Reintegration

Denial

Your period of denial will depend on how much time you had to "prepare" for the breakup. If it comes suddenly, you may have a period of shock, where you don't feel anything. Your mind goes into a state of denial to help protect you from the shock. You may say things like, "I can't believe it! I can't believe this is happening!" The period of shock and denial typically lasts from a few minutes to a few days.
During the denial period you will likely not be able to make much sense of the situation, nor should you make any major decisions about it. Depak Chopra explains that when something happens that we perceive as "bad" or "a problem," we tend to go straight into "constricted consciousness." We tighten up, go within, and may even want to physically curl up into a ball and hibernate for a while. This is normal and can even be healthy. This period allows you to relax so you can get to the next stage of grieving.

Anger

Soon you may find yourself feeling angry. You may be angry at the other person, at yourself, at others, or at the world. You may find yourself ruminating and asking, "Why?" You are beginning to come out of denial and see the situation a little more clearly (but not clearly, yet). You see the situation from your "pain body" as Eckert Tolle calls it. You see the situation from an egotistical point of view. It's all about ME. Why ME? How could he/she do this to ME? What did I do to deserve this? Why does this always happen to ME?

Before one can be angry, they must first have been *hurt*. Your anger is coming from a place of hurt. Someone has either wounded you or touched a previous wound that has never healed. The unhealed wound will be the most painful. This may be a "wake-up call" for you to finally get some help for unhealed wounds, so they don't have to keep opening back up. But first, you just need to get in touch with your anger, as you may not be ready yet to feel the pain of the *hurt*.

You may cry, scream, yell, and withdraw during this time. It is healthy to get your feelings out, as long as you aren't taking them out on anyone else, or taking them out on yourself. Depression is anger turned inward. Hostility and aggression are anger turned outward. Both of these states are unhealthy if you "act out" physically on them. During this period you may need to go <u>back and forth between inward anger and outward anger</u> until you can see things in a more objective and rational way. It almost always takes "two to tango," so you will need to take some responsibility for the breakup, but you don't need to take it all. Try to see both sides of the story. Don't get sucked down the victim hole.

Soon you will be able to relax a little more, and you will begin to come out of "constricted consciousness" and move toward "open consciousness."

<u>Bargaining</u>

Not everyone goes through the stage of "bargaining," but it is very common. After a short period of feeling hurt and anger, it's natural to want to be relieved. You subconsciously may try to salve your wound by having some contact with the person. You may feel you need to talk to him, see him/her, or at least write him/her a letter. You may feel you need to apologize and commit to never doing this again. You may feel you need to defend yourself. You may feel you want to inflict hurt and pain on him/her. You may feel you want to get "closure" with him/her. Whatever your motives are, it's best to wait a while before initiating contact or responding to his/her contact.

During the "bargaining" stage, people sometimes will try to figure out a way to get the relationship back. Many people will say things like, "I'll do anything to have you back in my life!" Of course, we know this is simply desperation talking, and as soon as you are back together, he/she will revert back to his/her old behaviors. Sometimes "bargaining" efforts pay off, and you are able to get the relationship back the way it was. You may go through the "yo-yo" syndrome for a while with lots of "on-agains-off-agains." Remember, these "back-and-forths" are most likely just temporary "fixes" and will not "fix" the real problem. Personally, I feel that once you've ended a relationship it was MEANT to end, and you need to trust yourself on that. Your second-guessing is simply due to your pain and anxiety. It is best to end the relationship by going "cold turkey," but it took me a long time of "yo-yo-ing" to get to this understanding.

Disappointment, Sadness and Depression

During this phase you will likely move into sadness. It is normal to feel sad and disappointment; after all, you've just experienced a loss. Even if you know the breakup was the right thing to do, it is still a loss of what you had wished for. You need some time to grieve your loss. While sadness is normal, depression is an extreme form of sadness, which is abnormal. Normal sadness will cause you to feel a little numb, a little off center, a little down, with a little less energy and drive, but you'll still be able to function. Depression stops you from functioning normally. Some signs of depression are loss of appetite, inability to sleep, inability to focus, inability to control your emotions, irritability, mood swings, and inability to engage in normal activities.

If your breakup was very traumatic for you and you find you are stuck in this phase, you may also be suffering from PTSD (post-traumatic stress disorder). The symptoms of PTSD are similar to those with depression, and may also be complicated by acute anxiety, flashbacks, and/or nightmares. If you feel you are suffering from any of these symptoms, please get some professional help right away.

In order for wounds to heal, they need care and time. If you've ever had a serious illness or injury, you'll know you have to take care of it until it's fully healed, or it can come back and worsen.

Many people stop their care when they begin to feel better, as in the common practice of stopping their medications. Any physician will tell you that you need to continue to take all your prescribed antibiotics even if you think you are all well. If you discontinue too soon, the illness or injury can come back, and this time may be more resistant to treatment. In the same way, you need to let your mind, heart and spirit heal. This phase can take anywhere from a week to several months. If it lasts longer than several months, you need to get some professional help.

Break the heart and its borders close, accepting no visitors until the worst is over.
--Helen Oyeyemi

How to Get Through the Pain

In order to heal in a healthy way, we have to go through our pain. We have to allow ourselves to really feel it. Why do we have to go deep inside our pain? Why do we have to go to that place where it hurts so much? Why can't we just take a pill or take a drink and numb it? Why can't we just replace it with a new loved one?

I once had a cut on my ankle that got infected. It didn't respond to the antibiotics and kept getting worse. I had to be admitted to the hospital and have three surgeries in six days. The problem was that they had to dig into the wound and clean it out. Not just once – not twice – but three times! They finally got it all out and it healed completely. Sometimes our mental anguish is like that. We have to go deep inside to clean out the pain – over and over. Sometimes it has to get worse before it can get better.

Yes, I know it hurts. It hurts bad. But as they say, what doesn't kill you makes you stronger. And this pain won't kill you! It's uncomfortable, but necessary for your full healing. I'll share with you some of the ways I've endured my pain. One way is to do your own "Gestault Therapy." Gestault believed as Freud, that there are three parts to ourselves – Our *ego* (adult), our *superego* (parent) and our *id* (child). Your child is the part that is hurting. Your parent is the part that wants to help the pain go away. Your adult is the part that is rational, objective, and mediates between the parent and the child.

Lay down and relax. First, get in touch with your child. Acknowledge its loss and pain. Allow it to cry, scream, and feel its pain. Then, get in touch with your parent. There are two types of parents – the strict, demanding parent and the nurturing, loving parent. The strict, demanding parent will tell the child she shouldn't be feeling this way and to "just get over it," as in, "just take this pill," or "you deserve better so go out and find someone new." The nurturing parent will be understanding, empathic, and caring. Be the nurturing parent and tell your child you understand her feelings. Tell her you want to make it go away, and you want her to be happy. Tell her anything you think a nurturing parent would say to a hurting child. Then, get in touch with your adult. Talk to your parent and tell her you know she means well, but your child must feel her feelings, and the best way to help the child is to allow it to hurt right now. Talk to your child and tell her you know it hurts, but it's important to allow yourself to feel your feelings fully. Tell her not to worry, because you will keep her safe. All she has to do is feel her feelings freely, and soon they will subside. Let her know that soon she will heal, and when she does, she will be able to contain even more joy. She will be stronger and smarter, and will be able to protect herself from being hurt this way again.

After a few times of doing this exercise, you will be surprised at how much better you feel. You will have acknowledged and connected the three parts of yourself. This is a skill that you will be able to use any time you have emotional distress in your life.

Another method that has helped me is to call on one, two, or three supportive people and vent my feelings with them. You'll find some of your support people aren't comfortable with your pain, and may have a tendency to become the strict parent. This is not what you need right now, so make sure you choose people who can be nurturing as well as objective for you. If they really care about you, they will be willing to listen to your venting at least a few times. You may need to keep talking about it for a while until you get it all out of you. Understand that some people may become impatient with the amount of talking and listening you need. Most people eventually become exasperated by listening to the same stories over and over. You don't want to become *their* OPP. You need to also be aware of the limits of their ability to remain empathic with you, and not take it personally. If you find you have exhausted all your support people, please consider getting a professional counselor and/or attending regular 12-step meetings such as CODA.

Another method that has helped me immensely has been getting in touch with my spiritual beliefs and faith. If you have a particular spiritual path, now would be the time to allow it to help you heal and strengthen you. If you do not have one, now might be a good time to find one. Be careful however. You are in a vulnerable state. Don't allow yourself to get pulled too deeply into a new faith or religious path too quickly. Take your time, just as you would with dating a new person.

Some of the benefits of going through pain and the grieving process are:

Learning important life lessons
Experiencing pain and realizing you can overcome it
Learning coping skills
Learning self-love
Learning how to ask for support
Creating a stronger faith (in God, in yourself, in your "gut")
Learning self-protection
Gaining a stronger spirit

Acceptance

Soon you will find yourself coming out of sadness and into acceptance. This is the state Depak Chopra calls "expanded awareness." You begin to look at your situation more objectively. You begin to see solutions. You begin to see ways you can create positive change in yourself and in your life. This is the most important stage in your healing.

Sometimes we don't want to get past our sadness. In case you haven't noticed, Western society tends to focus on the negative. The media would have us all in doomsday depression if we didn't know better. Friends and relatives mean well, but sometimes they just can't help themselves. People tend to feel more comfortable in negativity and sorrow. Staying in "pain body" can become an addiction in itself.

Scientists are aware that there is a positive energy flowing through the Universe. It is this positive energy that creates life, protects life, and causes evolution and growth. This positive energy force is what causes our hearts to keep pulsing. It seems this positive energy must be <u>much more powerful</u> than negative energy, in order to sustain life. <u>It is simply a matter of which energy we choose to connect with</u>. And each moment of our lives is an opportunity for choosing – one or the other. It is important to get in touch with your chi at this time.

There are many things one can do to create and sustain the feeling of positive energy. Contrary to the old hardwired theory that the human brain is fixed from birth, the recent studies of neuroscience has revealed that our minds are reshaped through repeated experience and thought. The most important thing one can do then, to have more energy, is train their mind to focus on positivity, mainly these three aspects: acceptance, gratitude and connection.

Acceptance of what is, the way things are, the way we are, and the way others are is the basic state of mind to <u>begin</u> to unleash our positive energy. Tara Brach, a psychologist and instructor of mindfulness practice, counsels students to harness an active "yes" through something she calls <u>radical acceptance</u>. "Our basic nature is loving awareness, but we forget," Brach says. "We disconnect; we perceive separation, and along with that illusion comes most of our suffering."

An excellent means of plugging in to positive energy, is to begin with <u>self-acceptance</u>. When people are compassionate with themselves, they automatically feel better and feeling better leads to more energy. When you accept yourself (with all your baggage) you will be able to connect with your true spirit, which is the source of energy.

You can "resculpt" your own brain through relaxation, meditation, and/or prayer. Positive energy lives deep inside each of us. We need regular, consistent "mental exercise" in order to bring it forth. It's amazing that people report only spending five to ten minutes in deep, relaxed, concentrated focus can give them the same energy as if they had taken a two hour nap. When you meditate, focus on acceptance, detachment and peace. Take some time to practice and experience this state each day – it will give you positive results!

Letting go gives us freedom, and freedom is the only condition for happiness.
---Thich Nhat Hanh

Healing

With "expanded awareness" and "acceptance" comes the healing stage. This is when you will actually begin to feel better and more open to others and life in general. You will begin to feel more energy and positive lift. You may go back and forth through several stages for a while until full healing has arrived.

Social support is extremely important aspect of healing. While you may not feel like going out and socializing yet, you need to reach out to supportive people in your life. Make sure you surround yourself with people who lift you up. People are either bringing you up or bringing you down. Choose people who support, validate and encourage you.

Gratitude is another powerful mind focus. Focusing on gratitude enhances the positive connection. Something people often say, "Count your blessings," is actually a very powerful statement. Daniel Goleman, the author of *Emotional Intelligence*, discovered that the components of energy are mostly present in presence. The most energetic people he found were "lively and engaged, extremely present, involved in the moment, often funny, yet profoundly at peace – even in disturbing situations." He also said, "You always felt better than before you'd spent time with them, and this feeling lasted." One of the words used to describe this magnetic state is *sukha*, meaning "a sense of completeness, contentment, delight, calm, and abiding joy regardless of external circumstances." *Sukha* is selfless in nature and connected to a greater purpose – which is why it increases through service to others.

Reintegration

Reintegration is where you begin to feel "normal" again. Your awareness expands to others, and you are more open to new connections with people. You start to feel more confident and self-assured. You are willing to expand your social network. You desire to get outside of yourself and join more fun and interesting activities. Connection involves three components, in this order:

Connect with self
Connect with others who give and receive positive energy
Connect by serving others

     Now comes Chopra's stage three – "pure consciousness." This is when you can start moving from consciousness to matter. You start creating ideas and thinking of ways to improve your situation. You may even get an idea you had never thought of before that makes sense. Reintegration is a time of feeling empowered and exhilarated! You should commend yourself for your strength to get through this grieving process. It takes a tremendous amount of inner strength to endure and heal from a breakup. When you feel this sense of empowerment, you will be ready to focus on your own life and move into <u>action</u>.
     Time does heal all wounds. Time removes all "emotional charge." Trust me, it does go away! The best way to heal is to believe deeply that you deserve a comfortable relationship where you feel loved and respected. Be aware than many people take advantage of those who don't believe they deserve more. Believe in yourself, value yourself, take care of yourself. Know that you are worthy of having people in your life who love you and respect you.

*   Time is a versatile performer.*
It flies, marches on, heals all wounds, runs out and will tell.
     ---Franklin P. Jones

Chapter Eight: 8 Tips for Dealing with OPP's

Tip #1: Fly in "V" Formation

Research shows that we are shaped largely by our interactions with others. Whether we have a long conversation with a friend or simply place an order at a restaurant, every interaction makes a difference. The results of our encounters are rarely neutral; they are almost always positive or negative. Motivation is based mostly on "VEE" – Values, Enjoyment and Empowerment. When I think of "VEE" I think of a flock of geese flying into their traditional "V" formation. Engineers have learned that each bird, by flapping its wings, creates an uplift for the bird that follows. Together the whole flock gains about 70 percent greater flying range than if they were journeying alone.

When you create space to focus on your own life, you will naturally be setting new goals. In pursuing your goals, especially difficult ones, you cannot afford the luxury of a negative thought! You must devote a huge amount of your energy to motivating yourself and pursuing your goal. You don't have enough energy to ward off negative energy and still pursue your goal with fervor.

If you feel someone is not giving you the support you would like in pursuit of your new goals, you should first assess whether their doubts are valid. Is it possible that these doubts are legitimate and that your goals are either too rushed, problematic or unrealistic? If this is not the case, and you feel that they are not being supportive due to other reasons, you should discuss this with them, but you should not allow their discomfort to stand in the way of you achieving your goals.

This being said, you need to know that the people who are close to you usually <u>do want to support you but don't know how</u>. You need to teach them how. You may need to give them the exact step-by-step process to use. Above all, I ask the people closest to me to be supportive, validating and encouraging. If they slip into negativity, I simply imagine I have a mirror in front of me and their words bounce off me and reflect back onto them. I state, "I only hear positives."

It is imperative for your success that you surround yourself with positive thinkers. It is difficult enough to be a positive thinker, so without encouragement and validation from others your progress will be impeded. Ask others in your life to "catch" you when you slip into negative thinking and self-doubt. Ask them to force you to restate your words into a more positive statement. Ask them to remind you of how far you've come and how much you have already accomplished.

Tip#2: Set Limits and Boundaries

To become who you are and let others be who they are, we must cultivate courage. We must believe that we are fundamentally worthy of love and acceptance just as we are. We must let go of who we think we're supposed to be. We must let go of who we think others want us to be. We must embrace who we really are. We must stay conscious.

Some of the greatest threats to our authenticity are boundary issues like the need to people-please. Being who you are means saying "no" when you really don't want to do something. But it also means saying "yes" to yourself and trying new things that appeal to you. The real you is stronger and more capable than you could ever know.

The way to set limits and boundaries is to first know what you really, really, really want. Once you are sure, you will be able to announce your desires to others with confidence. For example, if you want to join a gym but know it will take time away from your family, you can talk to each family member individually or ask for a family meeting. Then just say it. "I want to join a gym and work out at least five hours a week. I plan to go to the gym Mondays through Thursdays from noon to 1pm and Saturday mornings. I would like to know I have your support in this." Then ask for agreement and support. You don't need to go into all the reasons you want to go to the gym. Just the fact that you WANT to is enough.

Tip #3: Seek First to Empathize

What I have found is that once I focus on empathy, others do not have emotional power over me any more. I can love them despite what it is they are saying or doing. I am going to discourage you from trying to understand, analyze or figure out why people do what they do. I discourage you from trying to be a therapist, counselor, coach or fixer of any kind. This is a waste of your time and doesn't change anything. Do not focus on their problems unless they directly affect you. If they do directly affect you, state what it is you want and need.

Tip #4: Use Your Words Wisely

Your word is the power you have to create. Your word is the power you have to motivate, teach, heal, and succeed. Words can literally change our beings and actions. In her book, *The Right Words at the Right Time,* Marlo Thomas provides a wonderful expose of the words that motivated a variety of people who have achieved great things. She discusses how words have a tremendous impact on us. They can either serve to move us to action or to keep us down. For example, she quotes:

Muhammad Ali responded to a teacher's assertion that he 'ain't never gonna be nuthin'. Billy Crystal, Walter Cronkite, Katie Couric and Kenneth Cole also received words of discouragement that goaded them on to achievement. The right words moved Al Pacino to pull out of a downward spiral. Paul McCartney's words came in a dream; Steven Spielberg's came from Davey Crockett. Chris Rock's words, like mine, came from his father; Supreme Court Justice Ruth Bader Ginsburg's from her mother-in-law on the eve of her wedding. Rudolph Giuliani, Cindy Crawford and Gwyneth Paltrow heard the words that changed their lives during a moment of crisis.

Some positive self-statements come to us naturally, and some are much more difficult to fuse into our being. One of the words I often use is "intention." Intention is what we want to have happen – our primary objective – our true aim. When I wake up in the morning I think about how I want my day to go. I say "My intention today is to be safe, happy and healthy, and to complete one chapter in my book." My day usually goes according to my intention. However, sometimes it seems the whole world is conspiring against my intention. Lots of distractions come up, people don't do what they are supposed to do, things are delayed for reasons beyond my control, things break down and I have to stop and fix them, etc. I have to be flexible and patient during these times.

Usually however, what stops my intentions is <u>my own refusal to set limits with others</u>. People distract me and get me off my course by either asking for my help, or attempting to engage me in THEIR problems/crises/dramas. This is where I am weakest, as I am by nature a people-helper. So what I have learned to do (when possible) is to tell (not ask) others what my intentions are, and that after my intentions have been met, I will be available to them. By the time I'm ready for them, they have usually solved their own problem!

Sometimes, with certain people, I have to change the word "intend" to "insist." Sometimes it's okay to insist that things go your way. As long as you are not stepping on anyone else's toes, or harming anyone else, or neglecting to care for those who really need you, you have the right to insist on doing your own thing, i.e. getting to your appointment on time or completing your goal on time.

Make sure you reward and validate yourself for your progress. For example, if you have just accomplished something that was a challenge for you, pat yourself on the back and say "Wow, that really took perseverance, but I did it." It is very important to remind yourself often of how far you've come in your journey.

Life is a rush into the unknown. You can duck down and hope nothing hits you, or stand up tall as you can, show it your teeth and say 'Bring it on, Baby, and don't be stingy with the jalapenos!'
---Anonymous

Tip #5: Stop Apologizing

You don't have to be sorry for being yourself. You don't have to apologize for wanting something. You don't have to apologize for feeling something. You don't have to apologize for taking care of yourself first. So STOP saying "I'm sorry!" Unless you have hurt someone else, you do not have to apologize. However, if you have hurt someone else, even without meaning to, be sure to say you are sorry.

Chronically over-apologizing can be a dead giveaway that our confidence is flagging. Still, not all apologies are made equal.

Sometimes apologies can be very powerful. Apologizing for circumstances that are obviously beyond our control ("Sorry you ran into traffic") actually demonstrates empathy and increases people's trust in us. One study found that 47 percent of people lent a stranger in a busy train station their cell phone if the request began with an apology about the crummy rain. When no apology was given? Only 9 percent handed it over.

Tip #6: Talk Back to Your Inner Critic, Shame and Guilt

If you find yourself apologizing a lot, it's probably due to your inner shame and guilt. Shame and guilt can start early in our childhoods and become firmly implanted in our psyches by the time we are adults. We need to work very hard to re-write our scripts in our heads. Excess guilt and shame will prevent you from living your best life.

If you feel shame and guilt you probably have a very strong tendency to "parent" yourself. Freud described the three parts of our mind as the "id" (child), the "ego" (adult) and the "superego" (parent). A mentally healthy person relies mostly on his/her "adult" to modify his/her "child" and "parent." It is the "parent" part of us that is the "judge" and "critic." We tend to be far worse punishers of ourselves than anyone else has ever been.

Our "inner critic" says things to us like "You stupid idiot! How could you have said/done something like that? You screwed it all up and everything is ruined and it's all your fault!" Each time this happens our self-esteem goes down a notch and we feel less adequate and more inferior. At these times it is up to our "adult" to step in and give some reality to our situation. For example, our "adult" might respond to our "parent" by saying "You know, it was just a mistake. Everyone makes mistakes sometimes. Not everything is ruined, it's just a setback." You can take responsibility by owning up to your mistake, apologizing if appropriate, accepting the consequences with dignity, then move on.

The "parent's" place is to keep us from going too far in any direction, remind us of right and wrong, and keep us safe. It is to support, guide and encourage us. It is not to condemn us, make us wrong, inadequate, insecure, afraid, incompetent or inferior. Sometimes I have to get really mad at my "parent" and yell at it! I've been known to yell at my empty chair, "I will not allow you to shame me. I will not allow you to cause me to be depressed or fearful! How dare you rob me of my self-worth! How dare you rob me of my happiness and joy! Back off and do your job of supporting, validating and encouraging!" I always feel a lot better afterward!

You will succeed best when you put the restless, anxious side of affairs out of mind, and allow the restful side to live in your thoughts.
---Margaret Stowe

Tip #7: Remain Calm and Think Before You React

<u>Retain your emotional stability</u>. In other words, keep your cool. Every communication consists of three elements – the other person, the environment and you. You can only control one of these three elements – yourself. So the first key is to maintain your self-composure. You must take rational action, not emotional re-action. This doesn't mean you're expected to be calm like an East Indian Yogi. Just pause and take a deep breath before you respond. Remind yourself to respond first from your head.

<u>Treat the other person as a human being</u>. People tend to live up to what other people expect of them. Treat a person like a crazy monster and he'll do his best not to disappoint you. If you treat a person like a smart, sane, rational competent person, he will tend to rise to the occasion. When you treat him/her as a human being, with the respect every human being deserves, it may be enough to disarm him/her.

Communicate with him/her as a real person. Communication is the key to diffusing his/her hostility. You need to communicate in order to protect yourself. Communication may be impossible in person or over the phone. Text and/or email may be the best way, just be sure you think about what you write as your words could be used against you. Do not ever be impulsive or reactive with your communication. If you feel you cannot keep your emotionality out of the communication, you may need a mediator, therapist, or attorney to do your communicating for you.

Tip#8: How to Handle Resistance

Most people resist change. We are creatures of habit and the older we are the more set in our ways we are. It's unlikely you will ever change others much, no matter how much they love and adore you. They will only change when they decide to change. If you can't accept a person for who he/she is – move on. If you don't like where you found them, leave them there. And don't feel bad about it! Remember, you need to RAISE your standards, not LOWER them. You have a right to want what you want and need what you need. Don't apologize or feel bad about that.

Now I must admit, there are some people who have overly high expectations of others and won't settle on even one minor thing. This is over-the-top rigidity and these people will most likely end up alone. However, it's been my experience that this is a small minority of people. Most people have the opposite problem – low self-esteem and self-value – which brings me to this next section – setting limits and boundaries.

The last thing you want to do is push, cajole or try to convince someone to change. Pressure creates resistance. Simply let him/her know who you are and what you want. Then, give him/her plenty of time and space to handle it (or wrestle with it!). If he/she gets angry, tell him/her you will need to leave until he/she can discuss it calmly. It's perfectly fine, in fact helpful, to sometimes create tension in the relationship. You have to stay calm within the tension. It is necessary for change. There is always some discomfort with change. When you wait it out, you have the upper hand. When you stay cool, calm and collect, you win.

Here come bad news talking this and that, yeah,
Well, give me all you got, and don't hold it back, yeah,
Well, I should probably warn you I'll be just fine, yeah,
No offense to you, don't waste your time
Here's why
Because I'm happy!
---Lines from the song *Happy* by Pharrell Williams

The Four Magical Words to Deal With Resistance

There are people who have a negative view of themselves and the world. I call these people "impossibility thinkers." No matter what idea you present to them, they always find ways to justify why it won't work. They really do not want to change. They really do not want to do anything. They may *say* they want their lives to be better, and they may *complain* endlessly about how bad it is, but they will never let you help them find a solution.

When you attempt to help people who do not want to be helped, they will often "turn" on you. The easiest way to justify not doing anything is to discount the messenger. They may think that "the messenger is no good" therefore their message is invalid, therefore I don't have to do anything. If you notice that you are trying to motivate, help, aid, assist someone who will not take any of your good advice, you need to realize that you will soon be dealing with someone who MUST disrespect you and MUST make you out to be the "bad guy." It is their only method of resisting you.

Therapy offices are full of resistant people. It is my opinion that most clients could avoid seeking therapy if they would just take the good advice of their family and friends. This means asking at least ten people in your life who you know care about you, what they would suggest you do in a dilemma. Usually you will get a "common thread" of good advice that stands out. Yet many people are stubborn and rebellious, or prefer to find out things on their own, in their own way.

Some people are covertly resistant. We call this "passive resistance" or "passive aggression." For example, when you ask your son to take out the garbage and he says he will, but then "forgets" to do it, he is being passive resistant. The way to deal with this is to give people time limits with directives. If they do not do it within the allotted time frame, you need to calmly confront it and have a discussion about it. Set up a plan that both you and the other person can agree to in order to solve the problem.

When someone is chronically resistant, defiant or oppositional, it may not be possible to turn them around. However, if they are simply passively resistant now and then, there are strategies you can use to motivate them. One strategy is praise and validation when they are doing something good, or at least putting in a good effort. Another strategy is to say, "I need your help." These are the magical words with the greatest persuasive powers. "I need help" doesn't have the same impact as "I need *your* help." The word *"your"* is what gives the phrase clout because it makes the words personal. It is very difficult to say "no" to someone who comes right out and asks for *your* assistance. This phrase comes in handy when people really don't want to be helpful (like my teenage daughter).

Once you've done the mental work, there comes a point you have to throw yourself into the action and put your heart on the line. That means not only being brave, but being passionate towards yourself, your teammates and your opponents.
---Phil Jackson

Chapter Nine: Creating Authentic Power

Turn "Learned Helplessness" into "Learned Empowerment"

Martin Seligman, past president of the *American Psychological Association* wrote a book called *Learned Helplessness*. Learned helplessness is the theory that one develops feelings of helplessness when one feels that the consequences of his/her behavior occur independently of their action and are thus beyond their control. In other words, the reason I did well in this swim meet was because the top two swimmers were ill, or the reason I did poorly on this test was because the teacher only asked questions that weren't on the study guide. Therefore, we do not take any personal responsibility (credit or blame) for what happens to us. This is a major hindrance to one's success in life.

People who are in a state of "learned helplessness" often see themselves as victims. They see someone or something else controlling them, and feel helpless to stop it. An example would be a woman who discovers an ex-boyfriend is stalking her, yet she continues to talk with him on the phone. She gives her stalker "hope" rather than demanding he stop his behavior and/or get help from others to make it stop and get protection for herself.

When you notice a feeling of helplessness or powerlessness in a particular area, you should practice new self-statements regarding your personal strength and confidence. An example of a new pro-active self-statement would be, "It is my decisions, not my conditions, that determine my destiny."

Your 10 Signature Strengths

One way to overcome "learned helplessness" is to identify your 5 - 10 greatest strengths and stop obsessing over your weaknesses. Signature strengths are the positive traits you feel have brought you the most success and happiness in life. They are qualities you possess that you are proud of, and that others have complimented you on.

Examples of signature strengths are; 1) I'm generous, 2) My life is balanced and functional, 3) I'm debt-free, 4) I'm a caring, loving friend and relative, 5) I'm a high achiever, 6) I'm determined to get what I want, 7) I'm powerful and influential, 8) I care about others and they know it, 9) I'm a good mother, and 10) I keep my word.

If you are not sure of your greatest strengths, ask several trusted people in your life to tell you what they think they are. You'll be amazed at what they say!

One of the best ways to recognize your strengths is to replay the tapes on your mind's "video player" of the times you were successful. Go back to any and all successful experiences: a big sale; a good grade at school; a winning performance in the orchestra, the band, or athletics; a great shot on the golf course or tennis court; a time when you and your family experienced a feeling of love and togetherness; an event when you were recognized for exceptional performance. Focus on one time in particular and recapture the sights, smells, and feelings that accompanied success. The next time you feel self-doubt creeping up on you, replay this vivid, positive tape.
---Zig Ziglar

How to Be Compassionate Yet Detached

Our chi wants us to be alive, awake and enthusiastic. Our chi wants us to love and be loved. Our chi wants us to have the best life we could possibly have. As the saying goes, "All is fair in love and war." Love is sometimes like war. The Greeks created Goddesses of War because they felt that women were the fiercer sex. Women have the ability to be a lover and a fighter. Yes, we want to love others and be loved, yet we also want to keep our sense of self. To win this war, you must be a lover and a fighter. You must use all your strength, energy and endurance (your "chi"). You must claim your prize as rightfully yours. You cannot be lazy – you must work it until you either get what you want, or decide it's futile and pull out.

You cannot view the other person as the enemy. You need to view him/her as your ally. A true lover is a fighter who believes his/her desires are shared by her opponent. When you see him/her as your ally, wanting the same things you want, you will reduce the conflict. First find the common ground between you. Let the person know you and he/she are similar or even the same in some way. There are things you agree on. Hopefully you both agree on wanting a good relationship. If the other person cannot agree to this one issue, all your efforts will be sabotaged. Ask for agreement on this before you take on the responsibility of a relationship with him/her.

Sometimes there will be conflict. Sometimes you will not agree, you will find differences of opinion, or the relationship will change in ways that do not work for one or both of you. You must be at peace during conflict. Think "collaboration" rather than "conflict." Always remember that most people (like insects and animals) are more afraid of you than you are of them. People are frightened of the power you have to hurt them or keep them from getting what they want. Your three best weapons are your rational voice, your self-confidence, and your ability to create calm. Do not react emotionally. Use declarations, then back off. Your goal is not to rush a win, but to advance your agenda, little by little.

When you feel confident about yourself you will show up as more real with others. When you aren't self-conscious, you will be able to focus on others and show empathy. Whatever they bring you will not throw you for an emotional loop because you are strong from within. Your heart has a bulletproof vest. You are a steel magnolia.

Love is the ability and willingness to allow those that you care for to be what they choose for themselves without any insistence that they satisfy you.
---Wayne Dyer

Spiritual Empowerment

Staying calm and confident will assist you tremendously in any encounter. However, there will be times when you will have a particularly difficult encounter that challenges you emotionally. When you begin to feel the emotion coming up, acknowledge it within your mind right away, i.e., "I'm getting that awful feeling in the pit of my stomach. I'm feeling frustrated. I'm feeling sad, angry, like I want to run away or lash out." Then, take a deep breath and think, "Relax." If it is a serious emergency, obviously your chi will kick in immediately to assist you in self-protection. Your chi is always there for you, even if it is not a life-or-death situation. You can call on your chi to assist you any time. Remember, your chi is your core energy which wants you to survive and thrive.

What I do when I'm feeling emotionally challenged or vulnerable is first take that deep breath, then say, "Relax," to myself. I then imagine I am covered in a glowing white light of protection. This white light represents my God, and thousands of angels sent from the Universe to assist me. Thousands of guardian angels who swirl around me creating a beautiful white glow. I know they have me. They are here for me, to protect me and give me the strength I need to get through anything. I immediately feel a sense of peace and calm. I am able to respond to the situation in the best way I possibly can (at least not in a way I will regret later!). When I do this I am spiritually empowered. We always make our best decisions and act in our best interest from our highest selves when we feel spiritually empowered.

Spiritual Intelligence (SI), can be described as "The ability to act with wisdom and compassion while maintaining inner and outer peace (equanimity), regardless of the situation." Experiencing and integrating the skills of SI can have a profound impact on our energy, our awareness and our behaviors. Your higher self (your spiritual self) will assist you in any interaction. SI moves you from immature ego-driven behaviors to more mature, higher, self-driven behaviors. Higher level behaviors are things like listening to your inner voice, paying attention to what you are feeling in your gut and your heart, having empathy and compassion for others without losing them for yourself, drawing wisdom from your brain, and using your voice of reason. It is only when you are true to yourself that you can be truly present and compassionate for others.

SI can be learned through practice. There are many different spiritual paths. Your spiritual path is up to you to decide, and how you want to practice is your choice. I will give you some ideas that I believe will be helpful.

Peace of Mind and Stillness of Heart

We can always return to our deepest and highest selves by stilling ourselves till our heart—of its own weight—sinks below the noise of the world, below the advice of others, even below our own expectations. Once our heart is still, our mind can relax and we suddenly have the chance to hear what is natural. Once the heart is still, we can meet our true selves by practicing openness. Consider how a flower knows when it's time to bloom. Rather than preparing itself for a particular moment, it seems that a flower stays true to a life of leaning toward the light and to a life of continually opening in the presence of light. In the same way, we can move toward the presence of light (our God) and open up to its guidance. The life of the soul opens like a flower we carry within that is always leaning toward the light, whether we want to or not.

And then the day came when the risk to remain tight in a bud was more painful than the risk it took to blossom.
---Anais Nin

    This is the law of nature. Without struggle there is no growth. The bud must break its barriers in order to open into a flower. A caterpillar must break its barriers to become a butterfly. Everything living is worn down and broken open at some point in its journey, and when enduring that rearrangement, the seed that has been living within us, once given air, will grow out of that break. So stilling our heart and living a life of openness also means letting the unexpected break in our life heal in the light that finds us.

    Going deep within and going out above (which may actually be the same exact thing) requires a steady and quiet courage. When confused and lost, unsure what you believe in, lean into the light. Like a simple flower, the reward for opening to the light is that we blossom. The reward for leaning into the light is that we find our aliveness. And following our aliveness is how we meet our gifts and how our gifts meet the world.

    It has been said that when we pray we are talking to God, and when we meditate we are listening to God. Both are important – we must ask and we must listen. Often before I go to sleep at night I ask a question. I am asking the Universe, my spirit guides, my higher power, my angels and all who are there to hear me to give me divine guidance. I ask for the answer to come to me as I awake. It always does. I know that my soul is in connection with my higher power while I am sleeping. When I awake, the answer is clear.

Lessons From a Butterfly

There is a story about a man who found a cocoon of a butterfly. One day he noticed a small opening appeared in the cocoon. He sat and watched the butterfly for several hours as it struggled to force its body through that little hole. Then it seemed to stop making any progress. It appeared as if it had gotten as far as it could and it could go no further. So, the man decided to help the butterfly. He took a pair of scissors and snipped off the remaining bit of the cocoon. The butterfly emerged easily. But, it had a swollen body, and small shriveled wings. He continued to watch the butterfly, because he expected that, at any moment, the wings would enlarge and expand to support the body, which would contract in time. Neither happened. In fact, the butterfly spent the rest of its life crawling around with a swollen body and shriveled wings. It was never able to fly. What the man did not understand was that the restricting cocoon and the struggle required to get through the tiny opening was nature's way of forcing fluid from the body of the butterfly into its wings so that it would be ready for flight once it achieved its freedom from the cocoon.

Sometimes struggles are exactly what we need in our life. If we went through life without any obstacles or frustrations, we would never learn how to endure, and would therefore be crippled. As hard as it is to watch your loved ones go through struggles, we have to be very careful and thoughtful before trying to rescue them or fix their problems. Motivation often comes from our successes; particularly those that were hard fought and won. Unless it is absolutely necessary, do not deny others that kind of success.

Forgiveness

Forgiveness is a gift you give to yourself, although everyone around you benefits. It is the gift of peace. It is a spiritual clearing and cleansing. To forgive doesn't mean to forget. Don't worry, your subconscious mind stores all your experiences and will bring up the memory if it needs to in order to protect you. But unless you are in danger of being harmed, it doesn't need to come up for you. You can only "let it go" when you forgive.

Holding onto past upsets and pain will only serve to bring you down. Learn from them, grow from them, and then let them go. Do you think the butterfly is brought down by its caterpillar opening after it is out? Do you think the flower continues to hold on to sadness and resentment at the leaves that once held it tight in a bud? Absolutely not! We could not blossom or fly without letting go and forgiving. In other words, we have no freedom to become who we were meant to be as long as we are imprisoned by past injustices.

When you pray or meditate, say out loud, "I forgive (so-and-so) for (whatever). I give this person over to you and ask you to bless them and give them the lessons they need. Thank you."

I came to win
To fight
To conquer
To thrive
I came to win
Survive
Prosper
Rise
To fly
---Lines from the song *Fly* by Nicki Minaj and Rihanna

Chapter Ten: How to Let Go and Let God

Good morning.
This is God.
I will be handling all your problems today.
I will not need your help.
Have a pleasant and productive day.

The above words are written on a card a friend gave me many years ago and it is taped to the wall next to my coffee pot. I read it every morning while my coffee is brewing, as I give gratitude for my coming day. "Let Go and Let God" is one of the primary sayings in the 12-Step Programs. It is very powerful. Letting go and letting God means casting all your cares aside. It means trusting in your higher power to work in your life and others' lives for everyone's highest good. You must trust that the Universe is working for your highest good, and for the highest good of others.

You are not God. You cannot play God. God is the key influence in our lives and everyone else's lives. When we try to control other people's experiences and situations we are playing God. When we let go (give it over to God), it is only then that will we receive the spiritual guidance we need in order to get past the pain, the unknowing, and day in and day out challenges of this world. Letting go and letting God is not an easy thing to do however, it's a simple choice. You let go of the things you can't fix, you let go of the battles that really aren't yours, you let go of justifying your acts in order to get selfish gratification.

Letting Go of Control

As I've said, when you try to help, fix, rescue, advise, lecture or nag someone, you are really trying to control them. When you get stuck in this role, you become their prisoner of war. You are held hostage to their need to keep you locked up in a room called "OPP's." The first step toward your escape is to recognize that you got into this room because you were trying to control someone. They locked the door behind you and now it's up to you to find your way out, or remain their prisoner forever.

I hope you'll choose to escape. It can be done, but it will take some work. It may have taken years to get locked up, and it may take years to get out, but you can do it. <u>The second step</u> is to realize that you are not responsible for other people or their actions. You didn't cause their problems. You can't fix their problems. It's not your job.

<u>The third step</u> is to stop playing God. God is their shepherd, not you. God's directions and outcomes are the best ones, at the best time, for that person's highest good. God has a plan for your life, and a plan for everyone else's life. It may be that God's plan is for this person to be suffering right now, because growth cannot take place without pain. If you intervene and try to assist the person out of their pain, it may be going directly against God's plan.

Letting go and letting God means to allow other people's higher power to work in their lives. Martha Beck, featured Life Coach in O Magazine wrote an excellent article on letting go of control and giving people over to God. Here is what she says about controlling others. "How do you get your nearest and dearest to change their behavior? Love them unconditionally. And how do you do that? Simple: Stop giving a damn what they do." When I read this, I was shocked at first. What? Not give a damn what my daughter does? How could I ever possibly not care what she does or what happens to her? But the article went on to explain that when I show up as someone who doesn't care what my daughter does, and it doesn't affect me emotionally, it causes her to feel unconditionally loved by me. My love is not contingent upon her behavior. So what if I just let her behavior go and simply love her no matter what?

I started reciting this quote over and over in my mind. When Buffy called or came by with yet another problem, I would think of this quote. I stopped giving advice. I stopped asking her what she was going to do. I stopped caring what she did. Yet I still cared about HER. I listened to her, nodded in understanding, accepting what she told me without judgment. Sometimes I would say, "Is that so?" or "Really?" or "Wow, that must have been difficult for you." But I didn't try to change her or fix her. And you know what happened? She started sharing more of herself with me. She started being nicer to me. She started thanking me. And more importantly, she took care of her own problems just fine, without my help! Buffy and I still have our mother-daughter challenges. But they don't affect me nearly as much as they used to, and they get resolved a lot faster. Since she is the most important person in my life (and always will be) I am grateful I took the time to study detachment and letting go. It's made the difference between stress and peace, unhappiness and happiness, and "dis-ease" and "ease" in my life!

We Are All One yet Separate

For many years in my spiritual journey I was told that "we are all one." Therefore, I felt that if my friend was hurting, I was hurting. If one person is starving in the world, we should all feel bad. We are all connected in some way. We are our brother's keepers. I felt that world peace began with me, and I had a responsibility to make the world a better place. I was told to love everyone, do no harm to anyone, and always help someone in need. This was all good and fine, until I realized I was giving everything I had to help others, yet others were still suffering, and now I was too! I allowed myself to get depressed because there was way too much pain in the world for me to carry. If I wasn't carrying it, or feeling bad about it, or trying to help ease it, then I felt guilty. I felt a huge, heavy burden of sorrow and guilt.

Then I found out that God actually wants me to be happy! God wants me to learn my lessons, but ultimately the plan is for me to be happy, at peace and feel good. In fact, Wayne Dyer said that my purpose in life is to feel good! Wow – I didn't know how to do this! I realized here was another dichotomy. We are all one and connected, yet we are all separate and independent. How could I feel both at the same time?

I learned that I am connected to everyone and everything in the Universe by an invisible bond. Yet I am a separate being, with a separate mind, heart, and spirit. It is possible now to see myself as both together and separate. I realized I cannot attach my life to other people's lives. I am not them, and I do not identify myself with them or what they do. They will be fine, with or without me.

Release and Receive

Just as the two concepts explained above, "separate yet together" are seemingly contradictory, so are the two concepts of "release and receive." There are many of these dichotomies in life – things that seem opposite yet they are equally important. Releasing others to our Higher Power is a way of "Letting Go and Letting God." Once when I was praying and asking God to take a certain person's troubles away from me, I heard a voice that said, "Lay her at my feet and go on your way." I envisioned myself actually laying this person down in front of God's feet, and thanking Him for taking over. This is a vision I continue to hold on to, as it has brought me great peace and comfort.

To be fully at peace, we need to know when to release and when to receive. We must release others to their Higher Power. God has a plan for them. God has you and me and every other person exactly where we are for a reason. The reason, which we don't always get to know, is always for our Highest Good in the long run. We need to not only release, but *trust* that God is working in all of our lives. <u>We must turn our fear into faith.</u>

There is a balancing act of releasing and receiving. In order to receive what we really want, we must release that which we don't want. We need to create the space for something good to come in. When we release our negative feelings, stresses, fears, and problems, we let go also of our resistance to feeling good. We let go of our resistance to all good. We let go of our resistance to God's plan for us. Once we have released, we then need to open ourselves up to receiving. This is why the concept of belief in a Higher Power is so important. If we have no Higher Power, who/where do we release the negativity to? Usually we release it to ourselves and our loved ones. When we hold on to it we hurt ourselves. When we release it to others it can be destructive to them and to our relationships. When I *lay them at His feet*, I am free to go my own way and take care of myself.

Send him love and light and let him go.
---Line from the movie/book *Eat, Pray, Love*

Chapter Eleven: Creating Space for Your Own Best Life

Our deepest fear is not that we are inadequate. Our deepest fear is that we are powerful beyond measure. It is our light, not our darkness, that most frightens us. We ask ourselves, 'Who am I to be brilliant, gorgeous, talented and fabulous?' Actually, who are you NOT to be? You are a child of God. Your 'playing small' does not serve the world. There is nothing enlightened about shrinking so that other people don't feel insecure around you. We were born to make manifest the glory of God that is within us. It's not just in some of us. It's in everyone. And as you let your light shine, you unconsciously give other people permission to do the same. As you are liberated from your own fears, your presence automatically liberates others.
---Nelson Mandela

Self-Focus

Now is the time to focus on yourself. This is not being selfish, it's being self-ful. I have found the antidote for depression is action. Even if you don't feel like it, do three things each day that you don't want to do that will improve your life. Do not substitute another problem for this problem. Substitute with yourself. Get some support systems in place. Reach out to friends and family. Attend CODA and/or ALANON meetings. They will be your greatest source of comfort during this difficult time.

Just think about yourself right now. Figure out what YOU really, really want. Not what others want for you, only what YOU want. This is the time – if there ever is a good time – to be self-absorbed.

What Oprah Knows for Sure

"*Ye shall know the truth, and the truth shall make you free*" has always been one of my favorite Bible verses—one I memorized long before I understood what it meant. I've since learned that you can't know the truth until you're willing to know yourself—and vice versa. Knowing yourself is a lifelong process, with your biggest lessons often emerging from your biggest mistakes.

My biggest mistakes in life have all stemmed from giving my power to someone else—believing that the love others had to offer was more important than the love I had to give to myself. I did not think I was special, and that was my problem. My lack of self-respect, my belief that I needed a man to make my life all right, that was also my problem.

Then one day I got it. I recognized the truth that I am all right just as I am. I am enough all by myself.

The truth feels right and good and loving. Love doesn't hurt. Truth allows you to live every day with integrity. Everything you do and say shows the world who you really are—let it be the truth.

--Oprah, Reprinted from *O Magazine*

Finding Your Purpose

Your purpose will evolve over time. I have read every one of Wayne Dyer's books, and have noticed an evolution over the years. As Dyer has evolved as a person, his writing has reflected his deeper, more authentic person. His first books were mostly about managing your emotions, knowing that you are the product of whatever thoughts that you have, and becoming the kind of person you want to be. A few years later his message was more about not being a victim, not letting other people manipulate you, and taking responsibility for your own circumstances. A few years later he wrote more about self-actualization, fulfillment, joy and living at the highest level to which a human being can live. A few years later he began talking more about the process of enlightenment, peace and transformation. Most recently his teachings have taken on a more spiritual nature – the power of our intentions and our divine inspirations. I look forward to where he goes from here!

Brian Tracy, a well-known motivational speaker says that he was able to turn his life around in a dramatic way once he had a "magnificent obsession." A "magnificent obsession" is when you dedicate your life to a powerful and compelling cause.

Doing "who you are" means living your true purpose, desires and gifts. This is where true fulfillment happens. Examples of people who are doing who they are:

Oprah Winfrey – Oprah was often asked why she kept signing three to five year contracts with Kingworld to keep her long-time award winning talk show going. People wondered when she is going to get a "life." Her reply was always something like, "The show is my life, it is who I am, it is my voice, it is my gift. Why would I want to give that up?" Since this time she created her own network – OWN – which gives voice to who she is 24 hours a day, 7 days a week!

Steven Spielberg – After creating a number of blockbuster movie hits such as E.T., Jaws, Jurrasic Park, The Color Purple, etc., Director Spielberg was snubbed by the Oscar Academy (except for an honorary Irving B. Thalberg Award). He had always wanted to create a movie about the Holocaust and had held the rights to author Thomas Keneally's Holocaust book for a decade. He had been discouraged from doing this movie as others felt it would be too "depressing" and not "commercial" enough. When Spielberg started his own family in the 80's, it rekindled an interest in his Jewish roots and sparked his decision to make the movie anyway. In 1994, Schindler's List brought him golden Oscar statues for Best Director and Best Picture (it swept seven in all).

Mel Gibson – After spending $25 million of his own money to produce his movie The Passion of the Christ, Gibson was fired on by critics. The movie sparked more public controversy than any other movie of its kind. But Gibson was undaunted. His passion for making this film was greater than his fear of criticism. It turned out to be the number one box office hit of the year.

Authentic empowerment is the knowing that you are on purpose, doing God's work, peacefully and harmoniously.
             ---Wayne Dyer

Hope Is a Thing With Feathers

It is important to remain hopeful about your life. Also, you can instill hope in other people with problems. One of the best things you can do for others who begin to vent their problems onto you is to give them a sense of hope. Often I will say, "Don't worry, things will work out." I may say, "This is all a part of God's plan, this is happening for a reason, for your highest good." When I say these things it relieves me of the burden of having to solve their problem, it helps me to let go and let God, and it helps the other person to feel a sense of hope. Then I am free to change the subject or move away from the conversation.

Hope means that anything is possible. Anything you can dream, you can realize. Anything you set out to do, you can do. Hope is essential for life. Sometimes we are faced with situations that seem hopeless, yet they never are. I have found in my own life, and in the lives of many of my clients, that the antidote for depression is action.

Even after a tragedy we do not need to succumb to despair. By focusing on what you need to do in the NOW, or immediate future, i.e., get some sleep, pray, sit and sob; take a bath, you are assuming a future. Even if your future only encompasses what you will do in the next hour, it is important to decide on what you can do now to get through it.

In the wake of a catastrophe it often feels impossible to summon the least glimmer of hope, faith or sense of life's meaning. Hope follows action and action follows hope. Making plans in the middle of a crisis doesn't change the crisis but changes your feelings about it. It gives you a small measure of control when your life feels out of control. Each step you take on your road map to recovery is a step born of hope. Each step then creates more hope. Soon you will have built a place where hope can nest.

Throughout history (before psychotherapy) people have found relief and comfort in the immediate obligations and habits of ordinary, daily life. Talking about practical, immediate plans calmed people down during crises. Focusing on mundane tasks in the present can help build, inch by inch and then yard by hard, a pathway out of despair and into the fullness of life. The simplest act can have profound healing power. If you cannot come up with what to do next, ask for advice from a trusted friend, family member, therapist, minister or coach.

Hope is extremely important on your path to achieving your goals. Hope is what will keep you moving, working, completing daunting tasks, and trying new things. It is what keeps you stepping forward. Hold on to hope. Keep your vision of what your life will look like when you have achieved your goals. Do not worry so much about the "how-to's." The "how-to's" will work themselves out. Just take one step at a time toward your vision.

Hope is the thing with feathers, that perches on the soul, and sings the tune without the words, and never stops – at all.
---Emily Dickinson

Be Filled Up With Yourself

Object relations theory is about our attachment to people, places, things, and/or events. I remember at a very young age thinking that once I had that thing I wanted, then, and only then, would I be happy. Most of us learned this in our childhoods, especially if we came from high achieving parents in the Western culture. I learned it from my parents, my teachers, my friends, the media, television, and just about everyone I knew. Unfortunately, we have very few role models who tell us otherwise.

When we attach our happiness or well-being to an external object, or an "it" as I call it, (how others treat us, how others behave, having a boyfriend, car, house, husband, child, ideal weight, etc.) we can never really be happy. My family gave me the message that I needed to marry "it." So I tried that, and it didn't work. They also gave me the message that my value lied mainly in what I could do for others. So I tried that, and it didn't work. They also gave me the message that I needed to do "it." So I did, and did, and did, and "it" didn't work. I followed all the other societal messages, constantly trying to have "it," get "it," "be it," and "hold onto it." I found myself running around like a crazy person – doing, getting, striving -- doing, getting, striving. Yes, I did achieve many lofty goals that have brought me a great deal of satisfaction and pride. However, much of the time I was frustrated, stressed and exhausted. It didn't need to be so hard.

The problem with attaching ourselves to "its" is that once we get "it," we may be happier for a while, but then we must find a new "it" because we don't know how to just "be." It is like eating food. It satiates us for a while, but we will get hungry again soon. When that "it" that we worked so hard for turns around and disappoints us, we are often more unhappy than before we got "it."

Achieving goals is a good thing. Having hope for a better life is a good thing. Striving toward our dreams is a good thing. But it becomes a bad thing when we are overly attached to these things. Once they do come into our lives, they don't "fill us up" the way we thought they would because we cannot be "filled up" (or fulfilled) with external things. We can only be truly "filled up" (or fulfilled) with ourselves.

What does this mean, being "filled up with ourselves?" Isn't that selfish and egotistical? I was taught not to be self-centered. Family and society told me that I should be care more about others than I do about myself. I know they meant well, but they were wrong. Being "filled up with ourselves" is not about being self-centered. It is about attaching to ourselves. It is about finding our true self, our core, our soul, our gifts, our desires, our needs, our passions. It is about getting to know who we are, deep down. It is about being our own best friend. It is about being happy, satisfied, and fulfilled with our "beingness." It is a spiritual pursuit, a journey into ourselves, or one could say, knowing the "God" within us.

The happiest people seem to be those who have no particular reason for being happy except that they are so.
---W.R. Inge

Positive Affirmations are Your Magic Words

Affirmations are powerful expressions of thought that many people have found to have amazing impact on realizing their desires. Our thoughts create our power. Because every thought has creative power, the more you think a thought, the more powerful it becomes. The more passion behind your thought, the more motion goes into the thought and the faster it manifests. In *The Game of Life and How to Play It*, Florence Shinn writes, "Our thoughts, actions and words return to us sooner or later with astounding accuracy. The idea, then, is to think only on what one wants, and not dwell on what one does not want."

Many people ask a "higher power" for their desires to come true. If this has been helpful to you I encourage you to continue. Another idea, less explicitly religious, is to make "grateful" affirmations, such as, "Thank you for giving me the intelligence and skill to succeed in my commercial art business," and "Thank you for bringing me two new clients today."

I believe that our desires are within us for a reason -- a part of a divine plan. Thus there is no need to ask for things but rather to give thanks for them and know that one's desire is on its way. Create your own positive affirmations and listen to them over and over.

Repetition is one of the master keys to learning. The more you state positive affirmations, the less you will state negatives, as the positives will eventually squeeze out the negatives.

Here is the positive affirmation that I recite to myself daily:

I am a strong, confident, empowered woman. I know who I am and say who I am. I expect to be taken seriously. I expect to be respected. I trust myself and my inner guidance. I am worthy of being treated well by all those whom I choose to have in my life. I choose happiness and peace. I feel good.
---Lyn Kelley

Spiritual Practice

The path to peace is through spiritual practice. It is imperative that you take some time each day in your spiritual practice. This practice can be anything you choose, as long as it involved relaxation and letting go of all negative thought. For me, getting centered and at peace means connecting with God and the God within me. A spiritual practice or spiritual discipline (often including spiritual exercises) is the regular or full-time performance of actions and activities undertaken for the purpose of cultivating spiritual development. Spiritual development is about connecting with your soul, your spirit, or your God, whatever you perceive him/her to be. A common metaphor used in the spiritual traditions of the world's great religions is that of walking a path. Therefore a spiritual practice moves a person along a path towards a goal. The goal is variously referred to as salvation, liberation, peace, or union (with God). Here are ways different people engage in spiritual practice:

Writing in your journal
Praying
Meditating
Stating positive affirmations
Visualizing positive outcomes
Mental imagery
Progressive muscle relaxation
Walking outdoors alone, without headphones
Listening to peaceful music

Yoga
Rituals or sacraments
Religious study
Chanting, drumming
Painting, writing, gardening
Martial arts, such as T'ai chi ch'uan, Aikido, and Jujutsu

    I'd like to leave you with a couple of poems and music lyrics I read often and have served me well. I hope they serve you well also. I hope I've comforted you, educated you, and empowered you. Please let me know if you would like relationship coaching from me to help you find your strength and your chi. Thank you for reading this book. I want you to find real love. I want you to find real happiness. I want you to find these things in yourself, and I want you to become self-full.

Let It Go
By E.E. Cummings

let it go –the
smashed word broken
open vow or
the oath cracked length
wise – let it go it
was sworn to
go

let them go – the
truthful liars and
the false fair friends
and the boths and
neithers – you must let them go they
were born
to go

let all go – the
big small middling
tall bigger really
the biggest and all
things – let all go

dear
so comes love

Let It Go
Song lyrics from Disney Original Motion Picture Soundtrack for
Frozen

The snow glows white on the mountain tonight
Not a footprint to be seen
A kingdom of isolation, and it looks like I'm the Queen
The wind is howling like this swirling storm inside
Couldn't keep it in, heaven knows I've tried

Don't let them in, don't let them see
Be the good girl you always have to be
Conceal, don't feel, don't let them know
Well now they know

Let it go, let it go
Can't hold it back anymore
Let it go, let it go
Turn away and slam the door
I don't care
What they're going to say
Let the storm rage on
the cold never bothered me anyway

It's funny how some distance
Makes everything seem small
And the fears that once controlled me
Can't get to me at all

It's time to see what I can do
To test the limits and break through
No right, no wrong, no rules for me
I'm free

Let it go, let it go
I am one with the wind and sky
Let it go, let it go

You'll never see me cry
Here I stand
And here I stay
Let the storm rage on

My power flurries through the air into the ground
My soul is spiraling in frozen fractals all around
And one thought crystallizes like an icy blast
I'm never going back,
The past is in the past

Let it go, let it go
And I'll rise like the break of dawn
Let it go, let it go
That perfect girl is gone
Here I stand in the light of day
Let the storm rage on,
The cold never bothered me anyway

Comes the Dawn
By Veronica A. Shoffstall

After a while you learn
The subtle difference
Between holding a hand
And chaining a soul
And you begin to learn
That kisses aren't contracts
And presents aren't promises
And you begin to accept your defeats
With your head up
And your eyes open
With the grace of a woman
Not the grief of a child
And you learn to build
All your roads on today
Because tomorrow's ground
Is too uncertain
And futures have a way
Of falling down in mid-flight

After a while you learn
That even sunshine burns
If you get too much
So you plant your own garden
And decorate your own soul
Instead of waiting
For someone to bring you flowers
And you learn
That you really can endure
That you really are strong
That you really do have worth
And you learn and learn
With every goodbye you learn.

###

Thank You for reading this book!
If you liked this book, please write a review for me on the site you purchased from.
Then email me and let me know you've done it and I'll send you any of my other e-books FREE!

By Lyn Kelley
Published by GROW Publications 2020

Dear Jane Series:
Book 1: *The 12 Biggest Mistakes Women Make in Dating & Love Relationships*
Book 2: *How to Cure a Commitment-Phobic*
Book 3: *How to Turn a Player into a Stayer*
Book 4: *Controlling and Manipulative Men: How to Spot Them and Handle Them*
Book 5: *Self-Centered and Narcissistic Men: How to Spot Them and Handle Them*
Book 6: *Addicted Men – Drugs, Alcohol, Porn and More: How to Spot Them and Handle Them*

Book 7: *Low Achieving Men - Passives, Wimps, Dreamers: How to Spot Them and Handle Them*
Book 8: *Cheap Men: How to Spot Them and Handle Them*
Book 9: *Men who Lie and Cheat: How to Spot Them and Handle Them*
Book 10: *Emotionally Unavailable Men: How to Spot Them and Handle Them*
Book 11: *The Romantic Terrorist: Protect Yourself from Stalking, Harassment, Bullying and Threats*
Book 12: *How to Get Any Man You Want to Want YOU*
Book 13: *The 10 Biggest Mistakes Men Make in Dating & Love Relationships*
Book 14: *How to Break Up, Survive and Thrive*
Book 15: *Bad Dick, Good Jane: How Good Girls Get Bad Boys to Behave, Fall in Love and Commit*

Other Self-Help Books by Lyn Kelley:

How to Stick With Your Diet & Exercise Program
How to Motivate People! The 3 Magic Keys to Unlock Anyone's Hidden Motivation
The 7 Self-Sabotages: Why People Sabotage Themselves and How to Stop It
How to Become Your Own Life Coach in 12 Easy Steps
Stalking 101: Everything You Need to Know to Keep Yourself Safe
How to Motivate Yourself: Secrets of the Motivational Superstars
Online Marketing for Non-Techies
Thousands of Angels: Your Path to Healing, Empowerment and Peace
One Day She Woke Up and Decided to be Brave: A Woman's Journey from Fear to Courage

Thank You!

CPSIA information can be obtained
at www.ICGtesting.com
Printed in the USA
LVHW082122240820
664077LV00036B/2741